MW00513452

In the End, It's Faith

In the End, It's Faith

Letty Linhart

Copyright © 2003 by Letty Linhart. All rights reserved.

Printed in the United States of America

Publishing services by Selah Publishing Group, LLC, Arizona. The views expressed or implied in this work do not necessarily reflect those of Selah Publishing Group.

No part of this publication may be reproduced, stored in a retrieval system or transmitted in any way by any means, electronic, mechanical, photocopy, recording or otherwise, without the prior permission of the author except as provided by USA copyright law.

ISBN 1-58930-085-8
Library of Congress Control Number: 2003092957

Dedication

This book is dedicated to my nuclear family and to my extended family, Tom Herron (my spiritual editor), Carol Herron, and my North Coast Church growth group.

Contents

Introduction..ix
Living to Please God...11
Activities of Daily Living...15
Turning Points...17
The Living Part..21
The Avocado Tree..25
Being a Servant...27
Prophesying On the Mark..31
I Wish I had Known...35
Asking for Help...39
Looking in the Mirror..43
The Geese...47
A New Noah..53
No Maybes About It...57
Brand Loyalty..61
Abundant Life...63
God, Cats, and Chocolate Cake...................................65
Watching the Superbowl..67
What Do God and Fog Have in Common?...................71
Mansions and Butlers..73
Built-Ins...75
Reading and Listening and Grandma Moses.................77
Living Examples..79
Swimming for the Greater Glory..................................81
I am the Alpha, and the Omega...................................83
The Glad Guy..85

Spirit or World?...87
The Recliner...89
Christian Books...91
Heavenly Customer Service..............................93
Worry? What Me Worry?...................................95
I Heard it on the Radio.......................................99
A Convergence, Briefly.....................................101
I Want to Please God...103
Ministers, All..105
Do I Have a Leading?..107
On Lies and Lying...111
Meat Instead of Milk..113
God's Great Gifts..115
Servant Leadership...117
Pronunciation in the Body of Christ...............119
Living Biblically..121
A Higher IQ...123
Women and Evangelism....................................127
Taking Gifts Seriously......................................129
Happy Campers Inc...131
Proving We Love God..133
Standing in the Gap..137
Heeding Authority..139
Receiving...141
Finish Line..143

Introduction

This introduction explains that the working title of this book was "Living to Please God." Chapter One explicates this notion, and while it is not applicable to the new title, it really introduced the theme of the book. Here is the place to explain "In the End, It's Faith." That was a quote from the spiritual advisor, Mike Adkins, who cinched my new belief that I was born again. After a series of conferences, as I described in the book *Turn Your Eyes,* after intensive study in the apologetics literature, and after a lot of prayer—both by me and by the two daughters who led me to Christ—I was still undecided about commitment to Jesus. That's when Mike said, "in the end, it's faith." Certainty by logic was not something I could have. Certainty by faith was possible, and I found it. Since more than 100,000 Christian books were published last year, a lot of the titles I thought of were taken. Not this one. I hope that if my readers have lingering doubts about being born again, this little series of essays will quell them. The result is so worth it.

(A note: as in my last book, *Turn Your Eyes* I avoided lots of capital letters by using "he" and "him" instead of He and Him when referring to God or the Holy Spirit or Jesus. I think capitalizing the deity is an interruption in the text, and something we all understand, anyway.)

Chapter I

Living to Please God

Do I live to please God? If I don't, should I? What would it take for me to do so? I have many illustrations of what I shouldn't do, and a few ideas about what should take place.

My wonderful mentor (he doesn't know he is) author Phillip Yancey recently set me to ruminating about this subject. I asked myself how do I live if I live to please God? Where does a Godly life fall on God's scale, and what does it take to understand it?

Is my conscience God's thermometer, registering "fine" for what God, if I knew him better, would have me do? How long range and short range would be my aspirations, my ambitions, and my actions? Didn't God "hard-wire" us to love him and grow in his Grace?

If I live to please God, don't I become the person I always wanted to be? Will I be rewarded by life? One of my pastors, Mike Yearly, contends that God always rewards us (if eventually) for all the things he wants from us: courage, compassion, and all the rest.

If I follow God's word, will I rise above fear and resistance and find contentment in all my affairs? The odds are, I will.

Patriot, ambassador, and inventor Ben Franklin worked on self-improvement most of his life. He identified qualities he wanted to exhibit and added them to his life in stages.

In a much less stringent way, the program of Alcoholics Anonymous has led me to my own self-help program and from listening to others, I have a set of clues on how to live. I did a bit of that earlier ruminating in my book, *Clues for the Clueless..*

But like many long term alcoholics, I was furiously self-centered. In the tradition of the "haul yourself up by your own bucket" school of writing, I left out the obvious: God's directives. This tome, gentle reader, is my amend.

In my book, *Turn Your Eyes* I revealed my conversion to a greater understanding of God, of Jesus. I am careful to believe that my experience is not necessary for all those seeking continuous sobriety. My own 25 years in AA were marked by periods of agnosticism and then rudimentary spiritual knowledge. I grew in my pursuit of God, almost against my own inclinations. I believe, now, that God was drawing me even as I sputtered through life like some defective engine. Since my conversion my life is infinitely better and demonstrably so. A recent visit to my most skeptical daughter prompted her to ask, "what medicine are you taking?" in approving amazement. The answer, unsaid, was the Holy Spirit, not Prozac. By accepting Jesus as my savior and asking for my many, many sins to be forgiven, I had found a new eloquence in belief, it seemed.

This book continues to document the steps on my spiritual path. When I moved to California this past year, a new Christian, I realized I had to find a great church and a great Christian radio station. In Orlando, my station was an independent one, Z88, and it convicted and comforted me as it became part of my daily life. But imagine my delight when I found KWVE in Southern California and the Calvary pastors it features. God knew I needed instruction, and instruction I got from men who had spent up to 50 years in the Word. Teaching by these wonderful men pepper this book; by God's Grace I hope to be the salt.

I hope the reader will bear with me as I chug along the road to happy destiny and revise my earlier thinking that I can get there by myself, without the influence of a trinity. God in Galatians has left signposts, like billboards, to my destination:

Eternity in death, love, joy, peace, patience, kindness, faithfulness, gentleness and self control in the time left to me.

Chapter II

Activities of Daily Living

The most severely affected alcoholic or drug addict has lost all guideposts for living life. In their rehabilitation, they must fill out an ADL(activities of daily living) sheet. Typical of these is 1. Awake at 8 a.m. 2. Make bed. 3. Brush teeth. 4. Shower, shave, etc. etc. These tasks seem ridiculously rudimentary to any normal person. To an addict, they are revelations. Years have passed when they have gone to bed not at all or for several days; when they have slept in their clothes and their teeth are sadly neglected .They must learn normal living sometimes for the first time, sometimes all over again. Hence, the ADL sheet.

The one constant reaction to this new mode of living is a mood elevation. "It feels good to live like a normal person for the first time in years," commented Ed, an alcoholic. "It feels good to do the right thing" says Julia, a druggie who for years was a street person. Almost always, initial rebellion gives way to pleasure after a new regimen has been followed for a period of months. "I've simply shaped up" says Bob, a long term resident of a treatment center.

For most of us, God approves when we do the right thing, or our duty as society sees it. When we become adept enough at living an ordered life that we can become productive citizens, he lets us know, by helping us to feel better, by giving that hard-wired conscience a boost.

My own experience confirms this. I love living in the midst of order after years of disorder. I am a resident of a small travel trailer on my daughter's land in California. Housework, which used to overwhelm me in a huge home, is almost a distant memory. My ADLs leave me with enough time to do the things I wish to do and still be clean and orderly. I attend a 6:30 a.m. AA meeting most mornings, then come home, breakfast, straighten up my 33-foot home, and begin to write.

Since I am happiest when I am sorting ideas, not things, I consider this an ideal situation. And maybe, just possibly, I'm using a good proportion of my life for God. That thought gives me a tremendous boost.

I first learned of the pleasure of using my journalist's talents for Jesus when I volunteered at the Northland News, a publication of my church in Longwood, FL. It was so purposeful to write for the Kingdom that my move to California was followed by a stint at Good News Etc., a Christian newspaper in Vista. CA. A paycheck lured me away from that job, but soon I wrote the book Turn Your Eyes about my conversion experience and felt purposeful even when I was covering Powwows and Civil War Reenactments for the North County Times. I found the book fairly flew from my faithful fingers (pardon!) as I thought about my churches and my ministers and my Savior. It was a glorious time for me, and I'm finding my groove again with this little effort. How lucky we are, those of us who find what we love to do and do it. God is smiling on us, I'm certain.

And just incidentally, by living (and writing) for God I have a richer life. Aren't I, as my dear late husband used to say, a Lucky Ducky?

Chapter III

Turning Points

This last year I have been the coordinator for finding volunteers for a treatment center in Oceanside, CA. Named Turning Point, it houses alcoholics and addicts for a short time (usually after a suicide attempt and an insurance diagnosis). I use the term insurance diagnosis advisedly, because to seek reimbursement for their treatment, the facility must label their patients.

I can identify. Some 40 years ago I got one of those labels—about the only one of its day: chronic, paranoid, schizophrenic. The "chronic" part meant to me, and to some of the staff of my mental hospital, that my sickness would never go away. I groaned under the weight of that diagnosis until something happened, one of my turning points. You see, in living for God, as I see in hindsight I was, I joined Alcoholics Anonymous. It was, I am certain, divine intervention. Besides, it's a good story.

In my mental hospital, where I resided for several years, I became one of the patient "workers." My duty was the hospital literary magazine which was patient-written, created, mimeographed (!) and distributed to patients and staff. I had a hand in that somewhere, mostly in the writing part. My friend Anna, however, had a different job. A science major, she was the research assistant in the hospital's lab.

The experiment she helped with was typical of alcoholic research in the 1960's. It consisted of lowering goldfish in grain alcohol and measuring how differently they swam. (They mostly died.) Then, for a period when Anna helped, they mostly lived. It turned out that Anna, a fellow tosspot, was drinking the grain alcohol and putting the goldfish in H2O. The staff said "Off to AA with you" when confronted with this overt evidence of tosspotting, and she did, and I envied her.

She got out every night to an AA meeting. People picked her up and wanted to help her. They sent her cards and plants. "Why can't I have some of that?" was my reaction, and I began to go to AA meetings, too.

But it was the first meeting in a dingy basement in Lexington, Mass where I saw the 12 Steps of the program, now widely used, and fastened on Step 2: "Came to believe that a power greater than ourselves could restore us to sanity." Guess what was magic to me? Not power greater than ourselves (yet) but RESTORE. You can imagine that the psychiatrists and psychologists and social workers and aides and other patients focused on "patching me back up" or "helping me" but the underlying thought was, "She's a goner." These wonderful A.A. people used the word "restore." That was as good to me as a box of fresh-picked raspberries. Better. I was hooked, and I've been hooked ever since.

That "power greater than myself?" At first, it was my home group of sober alcoholics. In time it became a mystical presence, a "force" like Star Wars, to help me and order my universe. Now it is a loving God exemplified, like an actor in a Greek drama, with masks for Jesus and for the Holy Spirit. All one thing, After all, the God of Genesis (Elohim) is plural.

My pastor claims we can't understand the Trinity and have to accept it on faith because there are no analogies to three persons in one. I've just done my best in that situation and I cite my guru Philip Yancey who says the Trinity (quoting Dorothy Sayers) is like all creation with an idea, a materialization, and a recognition, just as God the Father is the idea; Jesus is the realization; and the Holy Spirit enables us to recognize the Kingdom. Like "restore," that does it for me.

When I said the sinner's prayer and took Jesus into my heart it was the next turning point in what had been a long climb upward.

As a girl in Cheley Colorado Camp in Estes Park, I climbed many mountains wining my "timberwolf" patch for my cowboy hat, and finishing off the season with a climb to 14,000 ft Long's Peak. That was a reward, that climb, but not until after "false summit" after "false summit" had convinced me that it was nearly over. Each time, another summit would appear, higher than the last. Finally, I signed my name in the Cairn as a climber of record in 1946. I had no higher place to aspire to.

Aren't my turning points like false summits? AA, then Spirituality, then God? As anyone who has ever signed a Cairn knows, I'm at the peak. My climb took 68 years. And now, I'm seeing that I'm living for God. In the past, I didn't know I was, even when I was.

Chapter IV

The Living Part

It is New Year's Day. I love New Year's Eve on the West Coast. The ball drops in Times Square at 9 p.m. and for those of us who are early go-to-bedders and early risers we can watch, then turn in and have a great night's sleep. All my previous New Year's Eves have been on the East Coast: Washington, D.C., Boston, and Florida. During my 18 Kansas years, when I could have gone to bed at 11 p.m., I didn't have a television set. Besides, by 10 p.m. I was too far gone to watch. Ah, the golden years of youth.

But the emphasis today is on "Living," or the Living Part. I would venture that it is easy to live for God in a monastery. Or a nunnery. Or even a retreat center, as the Benedictines sponsor. But living for God in the world? Where conflicting desires consume us? To do the right thing, to do the wrong thing, to be obedient, to be rebellious, to be spiritual, to be worldly, to buy and acquire and hoard or to tithe and give and many more choices that humans make moment to moment.

I'm writing this as I watch the Rose Parade, and I'm believing that God's parade is rather like it; every beautiful entry, it seems, won the Governor's trophy or the Judge's trophy or some such award. Just as God gives us rewards and favors for living to please him, "Seek ye first the Kingdom of Heaven and all things will be added on to you;" "I have come that you might have life and have it more abundantly."

I have seen these promises come true in my own life and in lives of those about me. We don't live to please God for the rewards we ultimately get, but we do realize them. And it is wonderful. Awards are fringe benefits. Living for God, like entering the parade, is blessing enough. Eternal life, worshipping Jesus in Heaven, seeing him face to face? When my eyes are on the prize, I can put a bit more in my offering and skip that tempting pair of shoes. I can set up in the venue at church rather than sleeping. I can avoid Howard Stern and watch Robert Schuller. I can choose Christian radio over secular rock and roll. I love reading and studying the Bible, rather than watching a suggestive or violent movie. I can associate with fellow Christians rather than worldly sophisticates, my former choices. I can be grateful for what I have rather than envious of others. I can be diligent in my duties rather than lazy. In fact, I can be happily square.

Living under these circumstances is a great blessing to me.

My earthly rewards from God are peace, order, and contentment. The long-term rewards, when I go home to Jesus, are incalculable.

Chapter V

The Avocado Tree

Outside my window is an avocado tree. It is sumptuously laden with lovely, ripening, green fruits. I need only to walk out my door, pick one, and let it ripen in a basket in my little trailer. Last year, I mentioned jokingly to my daughter, whose land and thus whose tree this is, that I would like to consider that tree mine. She honored my request. When the pickers came from the packing company, they spared "my" tree. The tree gives new meaning to the promise of abundance. More avocados than I could possibly consume hang from the heavy branches.

People who visit usually casually mention the crop. "Are those yours?" more often than not, is what they ask with a greedy eye on the fecundity of that tree.

I usually tell such visitors that the tree belongs to my daughter, which is true. That ends it. But if a close friend asks to have an avocado or two, I usually offer to fulfill their request.

Do you see a lesson looming here? God tells us that if we abide in his word, he will give us the things we ask for. God has lots more goodies to dispense than I have avocados, and I have a bundle. If we didn't have any other reason to learn God's strictures, that would be enough. To ask and receive.

But there are literally hundreds of reasons. We can rejoice with prophecy fulfilled, we can learn guidelines for living, we can find history lessons and heroes, and the list goes on an on. The word of God beseeches, teaches, preaches, and when the Holy Spirit anoints the reader the word is endlessly fascinating, prized, loved, as is God.

I once learned all I could about jazz. It was my music of choice. I have met many of the artists of that music and enjoy, to this day, what they do. But my music of choice has changed again. In my 20's and 30's it was the classics. After all, I was in Boston, there was an excellent radio station, the symphony, and abundant choices of classical programs from quartets and recitals at the Gardner to home concerts by very gifted players. Then, briefly, it was country and western music, then jazz. Now, I love hymns and contemporary Christian music. The hymns got a workout in my book, Turn Your Eyes, and I'm listening to contemporary Christian music as I write this book. As the hymns do, they spark ideas and comfort hard places when little to nothing gets to me from my waiting angel. (The angel guides me as a muse once did. I can picture him and he helps me and inspires me, most of the time .He has a direct line to the Holy Spirit, and I'm cultivating a direct line to him.)

Like the dispensing of avocados, God has a catch: if we abide in his word, really love him, study his book, go to church, associate with other, loving Christians, then we probably won't ask for material things, or at least not as selfishly. We'll ask for blessings for others, for the fruit of the Spirit for ourselves, for things that matter in the eternal scheme of things.

People who beat around the bush and hint that they might like an avocado rarely get one. If they're a good friend who has shown a real interest in getting to know me and who has shown not only interest but effort, then they walk away with a few avocados. After all, avocados are one of God's miracles. In the early 50's there existed a pejorative phrase, "He's playing God." I think it mostly meant that person was what is called today a control freak. I'd like to recast the meaning. If I seek and love God, he is just and shows me grace and mercy. I'd like to think I'm playing that God. Have an avocado!

Chapter VI

Being a Servant

Earlier I mentioned a great summer at Cheley Colorado Camp for Girls in Estes Park, Colorado. At the time my only achievement of note there was to win game night, when we used our minds. I was no great shakes at riding, shooting, and hiking although I comported myself adequately. To me, it seemed just like any camp, as it was the only one I had known. This year, I met a woman from Estes Park and mentioned I had gone to camp there and she was impressed. "Your parents must have been wealthy. That's a very exclusive and costly camp," she said. I demurred, relating that my father was just a country lawyer and we barely made ends meet. Not until that moment did I realize that my parents had sacrificed for me to go there; that it was their Kansas attempt to give me a pedigree. So many of the things they did for me I accepted as my due, little realizing that was their way of loving me. My mother ferried us to endless debate trips all over the state of Kansas and I never once thanked her. I realized that my three years on the Pittsburg High School debate team set my course for life, making up for a less than rigorous education. But I didn't realize the part our car and my mother played in all that. I thought she owed it to me; after all, I was winning trophies and being featured in the newspaper. Didn't that reflect on her? (I cringe to think of this, now.)

My parents, I believe, answered the call to be servants. I did that as well when I took my own girls to camp (in New Hampshire, not Colorado) and when I drove them to rehearsals and performances at the Boston Children's Theatre, and to the barn for riding in Concord, Mass. Servanthood comes easily to mothers. Sometimes, I guess, that was my only way of expressing love, as it was to my mother. I live close to my daughter and watch her doing the same, daily, with rides to school and lessons for her children. The difference is, hers is a Christian home, and her children value and honor her service. Or at least they have a better perspective than I did; they do, after all, honor their father and mother. I think I considered mine inferior and not to be honored, particularly.

On one occasion we stayed at a castle in Belgium (another sacrifice) run by a penniless baron and his very continental wife. The baron was a functionary of some sort at the United Nations, and my parents were awed. By then, I had played charades with Nobel Prize winners and dined with U.N. officials so the baron and I conversed in a rather familiar way. My parents were tongue-tied. Just one more instance to me that I was superior.

When Jesus washed his disciples' feet for the Passover dinner, he was foretelling a future cleansing with his blood and that is the essence of sacrifice and servanthood.

During my four years as an Episcopalian I joined a new, satellite offshoot of the city church. A young, up and coming minister, establishing himself as a servant, decided to have a ceremony where he washed our feet. We were warned, so when the day came we had clipped toenails and already-scrubbed feet. I can recall to this day how uncomfortable I was when this reverend, on his hands and knees, soaped and rinsed my feet in a large bowl, then filled the bowl again for the next communicant. As I could have predicted had I thought about it, hardly anyone came to the service. I did because I was curious.

I wore my Christianity lightly, then. As I studied for an upcoming wedding, I learned the concept of original sin, but also learned that the Bible was truth, myth, history, poetry, and literary expression. As the reader has seen, I have changed my mind.

I think that explains the "proper" churchman's view of an Evangelical, who believes the Bible to be the inerrant and inspired word of God. Of course, their view leads to the conclusion that we are fanatics. Our view of them is that they're heretics. This is merely an emphasis on perspective, on doctrine. I have often read in the magazine Christianity Today of a church father, especially in the Anglican or Episcopal faith, who isn't promulgating the word of God. No wonder. That churchman doesn't see the Bible as the word of God. He sees some of it as myth, or a historical view, now out of date. This is a caveat employed by the Evangelical as well, who thinks Paul's (hence God's) word about how the women should be in the temple, how they shouldn't cut their hair, were rules for then, not now. It's a short stretch to say the same of homosexuality. Then, not now, says the Anglican.

But there is never disagreement that Jesus was the ultimate servant. That unites us all.

Chapter VII

Prophesying On the Mark

With the advent of computers, Bibles online, and Concordances some interesting numbers are emerging from scholars and preachers. One example is one of the esteemed (at least by me) Calvary minister, Raul Reis, who like many of his fellows came to Christ during the Jesus movement of the 70's in California. As a result of all those years of teaching the Bible, which Calvary does, Reis drew some interesting statistics for his sermon this first week in 2003.

"In the 66 books written by 40 persons over a the 2000-year period,"...Peter in Peter II verses 16 to 21 gave an eyewitness account of Jesus at his baptism by John the Baptist, in which God said 'this is my beloved son in whom I am well pleased' and his transfiguration which disciples John and Peter witnessed and his ascension into heaven 40 days after he rose from the dead. Peter says that the prophesies about Jesus were from Holy men of God as moved by the Holy Spirit. Reis, in quoting, states that more than one fifth of the Old Testament concerns prophecies, and one third of those were about Jesus' coming to earth as a child, born of the virgin, in Bethlehem, coming to Jerusalem on a donkey, and dying for our sins, having been betrayed by a follower and deserted by his disciples, all of them inerrant..

Reis says there were 46 Old Testament prophets, and that the New Testament has some 300 prophesies, 21 of them from Jesus himself, that Christ will come again, this time to establish his Kingdom. He, like all Calvary ministers all over the country and the globe, believe that God whispered these prophecies into holy writer's ears

If it weren't for the accuracy of Bible prophesies of the Old Testament, I think I would believe it somewhere on the scale of unlikely to preposterous that Jesus would come again. But Peter wrote to dissuade false teaching, and he was an eyewitness to some pretty amazing things, and so who am I to be skeptical?

I will admit that this hurdle was the highest keeping me from believing in the inerrancy of Scripture. I don't know if I jumped higher or Peter lowered the bar, but the whole thing has moved from unlikely to possible to probable to certain.

Besides, I respect those prophets. In many cases they laid their lives on the line and were persecuted. Jesus told us when he was on earth that his followers would be persecuted in his name. I'm sure my Boston and Orlando friends will charge most of this book up to my brain softening in the California sun. My Kansas friends already know what kind of prophet I am. In my 1955 yearbook I summed up a "This is the Year that Was" article by saying about Rock and Roll, "it will never last." Still, I'm leaning on the prophesies of some really heavy hitters when I believe Jesus will come back.

As for the Bible being inspired by God, Reis really got out the cursor. He says there were 680 claims of inspiration by God in the Pentateuch, or first five books of the Bible, written by Moses. He finds more in the remainder of the Old Testament and in the New. Paul in 1 Corinthians 15 verse 41 wrote "Now the sun has one kind of splendor, the moon another and the stars another, and star differs from star in splendor." In an age which thought all stars were alike, Reis asks rhetorically, "How did Paul know that?" and answers, "God told him." To hear this sermon in its entirety, dial up Somebodylovesyou.com You'll get a kick out of Reis' enthusiastic style.

Chapter VIII

I Wish I had Known

Since I came to be a believer years after I signed on to social security, I often find things that "I wish I had known that, when." My immediate reaction to Mark 10:17-27, Jesus' words to the rich young would-be follower, was "Why didn't someone tell me that in 1965, when I entered my mental hospital? (To spare the reader from looking up the scripture, here is the NIV: Jesus looked at them and said "With man this is impossible (entering heaven) but not with God; all things are possible with God.")

I had to wait until 1975 when AA taught me that if I turned my life and my will over to God, then he could remove my alcoholic craziness, and any other peripheral craziness that had developed in my disordered life. I will tip my hat to one doctor at the mental hospital. He questioned me in a kindly way, "Mrs. K., we understand you have been drinking a great deal." But I shrugged him off. "No more than anyone else," I said, honestly believing it. After all, didn't I walk to a neighbor's house and share a bottle of scotch for lunch? Didn't I buy a case of beer three times weekly? Didn't everybody? How could anyone live through the assassinations, the escalating war, the rebellion at the colleges, without being drunk?

So I was put into the disturbed women's dorm and drugged heavily for a number of years. We all drank on the hospital grounds with bottles stashed in the woods and with visitors bringing thermoses of martinis. My husband visited nightly, until he got tired of my irrationality, and brought a can of beer. At one point he asked whether I enjoyed his company or whether I just wanted the beer he brought. I didn't know.

In my Encouragement Bible, a gift from my youngest daughter when I began my studies toward accepting Christ, is a poem I wish I had had five years ago.

Written by Dave and Jan Dravecky, contributors to this Zondervan edition, it concerns cancer, which overcame a particularly good friend. Marguerite (we all called her Mike) had breast cancer in her 40's and survived for many years until the cancer returned when she was in her 60's. One of my Delta Delta Delta sorority pledge sisters, Mike and I had roomed together on our reunions and I had corresponded with her in the sorority round robin letter. As we shared a room, she told me of her faith (she was a Deacon in the Episcopal Church and a hospital chaplain.) Two years ago, she died after saying goodbye to all of us. Years earlier, she had said "when I die, I'll die of cancer." If only I had this poem when she was going home. Here it is:

Cancer is so limited...
It cannot cripple love,
It cannot shatter hope,
It cannot corrode faith,
It cannot eat away peace,
It cannot destroy confidence,
It cannot kill friendship,
It cannot shut out memories,

I Wish I had Known

It cannot silence courage,
It cannot invade the soul,
It cannot reduce eternal life,
It cannot quench the spirit,
It cannot lessen the power of the resurrection.

The conviction that I was a sinner is daily strengthened by scripture and inspirational reading. A lot of my sins are sins of omission: I just didn't know. That's what the scripture shows me. I just didn't know. Now that I'm a new creature in Christ, I'm trying my best to live a Godly life. I live in the Word, and my heart is open to thoughts I once would have considered sentimental or not sophisticated enough for me to bother with. Furthermore, I like the me I am becoming.

Chapter IX

Asking for Help

I just called a dear Christian friend who had surgery a week ago. We chatted and I asked the inevitable question: Can I do anything for you? She said she was fine, but added that had she needed anything she would have told me, a sea-change from an earlier personality. I identified. Before AA, before Jesus, I was so proudly self-sufficient I would have starved to death before I asked anyone for food. Now, learning on an AA sponsor and on God, and learning my very own limitations, I am like my friend: I know when I need help and now, as she does, I ask for it.

When I lived in the country in Oviedo, Florida I sometimes got very ill and asked friends to bring groceries and keep me company. When my husband died, I leaned on my friends and they assured me that was fine. One of them missed work to be with me, take me home, and see to it that I was nourished when eating was the farthest thing from my mind.

I am getting into Orlando next week on a flight that is too late for a rental car, so I asked another friend to come out to the airport, a long trip, and drop me at another friend's house in her town. She said she was glad to do it, and so was the friend who was leaving her key under the mat so I could rest and have a bed, there. She even offered the use of her car. I have spent years with these ladies, and on the whole received very much more from them than they got from me. Most of them demur, however, when I say that. I have done lots of things for them, I guess, and I'm glad nobody is keeping strict count.

My mother, who had nursed her own dying mother when she was a young girl, was so self sufficient that one neighbor of hers told me, "she doesn't need anything from anybody." When she became ill in her late 70's, she had a full time nurse and seemed to sink into her care after years of not needing things. I came around as much as I could, visiting, going with her to doctors, but it was the home health aide she mostly clung to. I remember being jealous, but I was a different person, then. I remember thinking that years of repressed neediness had erupted like a volcano for her. I'm glad I'm parceling out my neediness one crisis at a time.

Jesus often pointed out to his followers that of himself he did nothing. "It is the father who does the works," and that means that another example he sets for us is to live God's will, and to lean on help. Don't you suppose that the "macho cowboy/John Wayne/self-sufficient person image" has infected our culture, and that's just another reason for rejecting help from God? Increasingly, macho athletes are revealing their love of Jesus. Terry Bradshaw, for example, pulled out a Bible on a national sports show on television. God's great commission: to spread the Gospel to all the world, has a powerful ally there.

When he walked the earth, Jesus was repeatedly asked for healing. So much so that to get his attention, the friends of the sick resorted to measures like lowering the infirm one through the roof of a home Jesus was visiting. We know only of a few spectacular miracles in the Gospels, but allusions such as "many were healed" dot the page, implying that we didn't get the whole skinny. And of course, with his death Jesus was our ultimate help, guaranteeing us all relief from our sins, and eternity in Heaven.

Many of the familiar hymns we sing in church services in America range from polite "please pleas" to beseeching. "O Come O Come Emmanuel, and ransom captive Israel," is non-sectarian enough to be sung in our public schools and yet is a fine example of the genre. "God our ever present help in times of trouble" is another. How about "He Lifted Me?"

To digress, at our megachurch, the location of the brow varies among the staff. To be clearer, Steve Redden preached this weekend, and he is a self-admitted lowbrow, chiding last week's pastor, Mike Yearley, for his highbrow vocabulary. Mike has even been known to manufacture words to prove a point. Our pastor. Larry Osborne is the only sane Osborne on television (when he appears) and because of the spectrum, everyone from intellectual snob to plain-talking guy is happy, enriched, and therefore helped.

(Dawn has come to my hillside in a spectacular array of reds and roses and purples and blues. God really rewards us here in Southern California. We couldn't ask for more. But, of course, we do.)

Chapter X

Looking in the Mirror

As I sit at my desk/table in my tiny trailer, I look directly into a full-length, beveled mirror. This place in its heyday was quite something: stained glass, carved wood and all. Because my nearsighted eyes don't perceive detail at a distance, I look pretty good in that mirror. The effect is that of a picture taken through gauze. If I counted on that mirror to tell me what I look like, I'd be pretty happy with my appearance. The mirror does not record the ravages of gravity. I see myself behind my laptop, shoulders up to a fuzzy face. I think everyone should have a mirror like mine.

And we do. God sees us as beautiful. When we look into the eyes of Jesus for the first time, our reflection will be even better than mine in my mirror.

I just went to an Epiphany party, and one of the guests asked what I had done to look younger. I didn't know at the time, but I guess it's my mirror. I'm trying to grow into the reflection that God has provided.

There is a wonderful fable about a prince in a faraway land who was born with a crooked back. His father, heartbroken, consulted the local wise man, who said have the best sculptor make a statue of the prince, but with a straight back. The king did that, and placed the statue in the midst of the prince's garden, where he played daily. Years went by, and the prince grew straighter and straighter, until finally he matched the statue.

I hope someone reading this can tell me the name of the 40's movie where two accident victims, disfigured, saw each other as beautiful. Robert Cummings was the male, and I remember Barbara Stanwick as the female, but not with certainty. The upshot of this example is that through the magic of special effects and makeup, their scars and brokenness were healed when they looked into the eyes of love.

As often happens, sociologists have endorsed what my father called "horse sense" and what Proverbs teaches. They call the theory, appropriately enough for this chapter, "The Mirror Effect." As horse sense and Proverbs say, we grow in the image our companions have of us. If we join a gang, we become more gang-like, lawless and even sometimes murderous. If we socialize with other Christians, we try to be more Christ-like, for we are seen as a Christian.

There is a catch to the latter, however. Many "earth people" (a term used by alcoholics to describe others) see Christians at best priggish and at worst hypocritical. Senator John Edwards has declared his candidacy for the Presidency, championing the "regular people." I'm afraid that some of those have a dim view of Christians.

But now that I am one, I appreciate them. My Growth Group is peopled with the usual spectrum of belief, but all are sincerely trying to grow in the image of God, as the Apostle Paul tells us to do. Talk about the Mirror Effect! To strive for the fruit of the Spirit. To always love. To seek and give peace. To relish life with joy. To be disciplined enough to do our duty, to live up to our obligations. To think on the things that Paul says in Philippians are worth-while: truth, nobility ,right, purity, admirable, excellent, or praiseworthy.

To live with the love that God describes in 1 Corinthians 13:9-21. What a mirror the Word provides.

My dear friend Lawrie called yesterday in great travail. She had had an ugly confrontation with a relative, the second of its kind, and while each had ended amicably they reminded her of many such abusive moments with her late father. "Unforgiving, she wanted to send a message that she wouldn't be treated that way. Her method, I told her, was to invite more of the confrontations she hated. "I've got boundaries, and I want to make them clear," she insisted. I confess that I bristled a bit at the notion of "boundaries" which is one of those psychological fads that come and go, like inner children. "Boundaries are fine, but soften your communication so as not to invite more confrontations. Tell Dan that you have a residual childhood horror of sessions like that which turn ugly." That was my feeling, somehow having God show me that what to Dan was "clearing the air" to Lawrie was abuse. Dan probably had no idea about her reaction which was to sob for two hours.

I secretly said that if we live with forgiveness, to dead fathers and other relatives, then boundaries are a false concept. I'm with Paul: "if your enemy is hungry, feed him. If he is thirsty, give him something to drink. In doing this, you will heap burning coals on his head." True, a sociopath here and there will say he got the best of me, but most will respond positively.

My friend Sherry after counseling about "boundaries" was fired from her job and got divorced. Is something going wrong here? I don't want to carp, but the psychologizing of America is an affront to those of us who believe the Bible. I will add that I went to a counselor all the time I lived in Orlando and received a great deal of help with my living problems. She was blessedly free of jargon and full of common sense. I'm looking for a Christian counselor now that I've moved to California and become a believer. As one friend wisely noted, "we need all the help we can get."

As I shut my computer this morning and turn away from my very own mirror, I realize I've sped far afield from the original premise of this chapter. But I've been seeing my reflection all along......

Chapter XI

The Geese

There was once a man who didn't believe in God, and he didn'thesitate to let others know how he felt about religion and religious holidays, like Christmas. His wife, however, did believe, and she raised their children to also have faith in God and Jesus, despite his disparaging comments.

One snowy Christmas Eve, his wife was taking their children to a Christmas Eve service in the farm community in which they lived. She asked him to come, but he refused.

"That story is nonsense!" he said. "Why would God lower Himself to come to Earth as a man? That's ridiculous!"

So she and the children left, and he stayed home. A while later, the winds grew stronger and the snow turned into a blizzard. As the man looked out the window, all he saw was a blinding snowstorm. He sat down to relax before the fire for the evening. Then he heard a loud thump. Something had hit the window. Then another thump. He looked out, but couldn't see more than a few feet. When the snow let up a little, he ventured outside to see what could have been beating on his window.

In the field near his house he saw a flock of wild geese. Apparently they had been flying south for the winter when they got caught in the snowstorm and couldn't go on. They were lost and stranded on his farm, with no food or shelter. They just flapped their wings and flew around the field in low circles, blindly and aimlessly. A couple of them had flown into his window, it seemed.

The man felt sorry for the geese and wanted to help them. The barn would be a great place for them to stay, he thought. It's warm and safe; surely they could spend the night and wait out the storm. So he walked over to the barn and opened the doors wide, then watched and waited, hoping they would notice the open barn and go inside. But the geese just fluttered around aimlessly and didn't seem to notice the barn or realize what it could mean for them.

The man tried to get their attention, but that just seemed to scare them and they moved further away. He went into the house and came out with some bread, broke it up, and made a breadcrumbs trail leading to the barn. They still didn't catch on. Now he was getting frustrated. He got behind them and tried to shoo them toward the barn, but they only got more scared and scattered in every direction except toward the barn. Nothing he did could get them to go into the barn where they would be warm and safe. "Why don't they follow me?!" he exclaimed. "Can't they see this is the only place where they can survive the storm?" He thought for a moment and realized that they just wouldn't follow a human. "If only I were a goose, then I could save them," he said out loud.

Then he had an idea. He went into barn, got one of his own geese, and carried it in his arms as he circled around behind the flock of wild geese. He then released it. His goose flew through the flock and straight into the barn and one by one the other geese followed it to safety.

He stood silently for a moment as the words he had spoken a few minutes earlier replayed in his mind: "If only I were a goose, then I could save them!" Then he thought about what he had said to his wife earlier. "Why would God want to be like us? That's ridiculous!"

Suddenly it all made sense.That is what God had done. We were like the geese - blind, lost, perishing. God had His Son become like us so He could show us the way and save us. That was the meaning of Christmas, he realized. As the winds and blinding snow died down, his soul became quiet and pondered this wonderful thought.

Suddenly he understood what Christmas was all about, why Christ had come. Years of doubt and disbelief vanished like the passing storm. He fell to his knees in the snow, and prayed his first prayer: "Thank You, God, for coming in human form to get me out of the storm!"

Isn't that a wonderful little parable? Jesus taught in parables, the universal language form. Throughout the New Testament he illustrated God's forgiveness, justice, understanding, and love with ordinary stories about ordinary people—with sometimes a king or two as the protagonist.

When I was a teacher I tried to use illustrations, as he did. I had to convince scores of junior-college English composition students of the need to write a capsule plot summary in their book reviews. The curriculum wanted analysis, not detailed plot "first this, then this, then this, etc." Of course, their analysis had to be supported by instances from the book, movie, or song, but most beginners don't get that.

I decided I would give them an exercise, with a reward: "I'll give 10 points toward anyone who can tell me what this plot summary refers to. It could be a movie, a song, a TV show, or a book. A man comes to on a tropical island after days of indolent drinking; he muses that he doesn't remember getting a tattoo and after first blaming a woman says that his state is his own responsibility." Out of a class of 30, 14 wrote Jimmy Buffett's *Margaritaville* and were given 10 points in a point/grade system. I thought later that song is a parable. Most folk music is as well.

Many of the psalms were written to remind the Israelites that if they strayed from God there would be dire consequences. Often these songs were committed to memory and sung around a fire; the Biblical equivalent of "You are my sunshine,." Or "Ninety-nine bottles of beer on the wall."

My dear grandson Caleb sings Veggie Tales songs, such as "God is Big" and I can see that a whole generation will know songs about God again.

Songs attract us today. I did my best to discuss that in my book *Turn Your Eyes*. Praise songs sometimes crowd out the grand old traditional hymns in worship services around the country. I'm so pleased with my church which offers an alternative traditional service with piano and hymns on Sunday morning. We also have a leader in our Over 55 singers who plays old hymns; patients in nursing homes, our audience, are given large print books to sing along. Often, as they join into the old time songs, the patients become teary and some even sob audibly. These songs have the power to touch hearts.

When the late Madelyn Murray O'Hare took God out of the public schools, there were unintended consequences. The music teachers, who, in the 50's taught us "This is My Father's World" "In the Garden," and even "Amazing Grace" couldn't do that anymore. Since that was the chief way that school children learned the Gospel story that Christ died for us and redeemed us, songs like "My Reedemer Livith" which I learned in 7th grade,disappeared. School children

can pray in silence, but unless they have a Christian back-
ground, they really don't know much about whom they're
praying to.

I recently heard a group of young performers present a
program they give to elementary schools throughout the
country which teaches those students, in song, Bible heroes and gospel lessons. Primary Focus is the group, and it
operates seven entertaining teams which present the Jesus
story. The headquarters are close in Santee, California, and
the entertainers ranging in age from 18 to 22 are giving a
year or two of their lives to do this work for the great sum
of $15 per week. Because they're peppy, personable and
current, they are sneaking Jesus back into the public schools.
Their founder, a former pastor, told us that every school
they have visited for the past two years asks them to come
back. I don't know about you, but I've put them on my
donations list. The group was only an idea for twelve years
until Rich DeVoss, the founder of Amway and well-known
Christian philanthropist seeded the 12 million dollars to
get the program started. Now, would somebody please con-
vert Warren Buffet and Bill Gates. We could use the money
for the Kingdom.

That reminds me in a roundabout way of a conversation I overheard between my first husband and Clint
Murcheson, then the richest man in America.. The latter
had hired him, an MIT Professor of Electrical Engineering,
to evaluate a new radio discovery which he went to California and did. He wrote a report. Murcheson called him at
home and said "should I invest?" Bob said it's up to your
advisors. It's a new technology but I don't have any way of
knowing whether it can be exploited financially."
My husband was polite, direct, and non-committal. I asked
him later if Murcheson hadn't awed him. "Why should he?"

asked Bob. I, who was almost struck dumb when the phone said "tell him Clint Murcheson is calling", kept my awe to myself.

Chapter XII

A New Noah

Increasingly, those in religious and quasi-religious circles believe we are in the End Times. Citing Bible prophecy and Bible history, they say God destroys things and has promised to do so when nations turn away from him. Heaven knows we have turned away.

Last time, it was a flood. This time, according to many, it is a firebomb, probably nuclear. I hope somewhere God has found a faithful and God-fearing man to build a space ship to connect with the space station and preserve our civilization. Our new Noah can learn to build a space ship. The original didn't have a clue about how to build and fill an ark. It took Noah 300 years or so; the new Noah might get that much time today, but it isn't likely. I hope that someone, somewhere, is far along on an escape ship and I hope he will read this and contact me if he is. I might pay for passage. All I have.

Other civilizations have toppled due to alien hordes and have not been well preserved. I suggest a government program to put all our knowledge of science, the country's long suit, on CD Roms and to pack a computer. Then, blast off.

Of course, I could be raptured. A lot of people believe in that as well, That poses a question. If all the people surveyed as born again are taken up to heaven before the tribulation, what happens to civilization? If the President is a believer, and is taken up, what will happen to the government? Perhaps a test for election will be agnosticism.

Now I know this speculation would be regarded as the ravings of a chronic, paranoid schizophrenic which was, in fact, my diagnosis in 1964 after a ton of drugs and alcohol. In my mental hospital in Belmont, Mass, there were many, many with my diagnosis. One young man, after 8 years of treatment, was found to be hypoglycemic, or behaving strangely to low blood sugar. Probably all 200 with my diagnosis had contributing factors, as I did, like bottles and drugs in the woods. The science of mental illness in the 60's was at best inexact. Besides, the paragraphs under discussion were typed with my tongue firmly in my cheek.

Fortunately, patient care has changed. However, it is still necessary for patients in mental facilities to receive diagnoses for insurance purposes. Often, these diagnoses are a kind of quantum effect. Leading to "because I am bi-polar, I am erratic" kind of reasoning, solidifying what might have been occasional acting out. I wonder why no one has insisted that these labels are inhumane. I'd like to pause a moment and suggest that in the new earth labels go.

I once wrote that my years in my mental hospital taught me to endure the unendurable. I have a more recent example. My late husband and I had a reservation for the millennium celebration in a seaside hotel in Haiti. We spent the last of December '99 in the Dominican Republic, then crossed the border into Haiti. Once there, we learned, alas, that public transportation was a "tap-tap"; a pickup truck with no shock absorbers, rimmed with rails and full of comestibles, including live chickens who thought my red leather jacket was a toilet. The 20 or so riders jostled one another over the most miserable dirt, pock-marked road from the border to Port au Priince, a distance of some 45 miles which took five hours. Slowing us down were pit stops. When a passenger felt the call of nature, he shrieked "pee pee" at the driver who miraculously heard him over the din of the engine and stopped. The aggrieved person hopped down, went into the bushes, and came out much relieved. After two hours of this, my husband was ready to get out and take his chances on something better coming along. I was barely discomfited. It was so much easier to stand than cold packs for a weekend had been. Eventually, Dan got into a conversation with the one person on the truck who spoke English, and who told us everyone thought we were missionaries.

Who else would put up with this seemed to be the consensus. We were the only two white faces in the truck, and in almost all the rest of Haiti. We managed a flight back in a small airplane, skipping the tap-tap. Interestingly enough, the attendant at the airport didn't accept our travelers checks; she had never seen them before. When the pilot came in, he explained they were like money and she could take them. She was uniformed, coiffed, and attractive and clueless. I'm pretty sure the new Noah isn't building an escape ship in Haiti.

In fact, I'd bet that the new ark is being built in California, Florida, or Arizona. When Kennedy Space Center downsized, the unemployed rocket scientists loved Florida and stayed there in various capacities, one of them being building waterbeds. It's a short step from that to arks.

The hilltop hotel in Haiti was glorious, and we had CNN in our room, watching Y2K celebrations all over the globe. The ocean roared outside, and the clean linens and antique furniture seemed a millennium away from the trip to get there. God just wanted to see if we could stand the journey, then rewarded us. Life is like that, isn't it?

Chapter XIII

No Maybes About It

Jesus never said "I may be the light of the world." He never said "No one comes to the Father except through a committee." He never said "Possibly I am the way, the truth, and the life." No, not at all. Jesus had authority. He taught as one with empowerment, and said he did all things through the Father who strengthened him. He even said, "If you have seen me, you have seen the Father." As he was preaching, I wish,O I wish, I had been there. I'll bet that years of struggling and doubt would have been erased in a New York minute.

His words in red in my King James Bible just didn't pack the same wallop. I expect that had something to do with me. I read the Bible as literature in school, but there was no wallop there, either. Years later I found, when I entertained the Holy Spirit, that the words in the Bible went straight to my heart. And because God lives in me I have some authority, too.

You see, I've become dependent on God for advice and for companionship and for guidance and for aid and for comfort. When the door in my little 5th Wheel swings down and punctures my shin, I no longer say "god damn it," I pray for the hurt to be relieved. When I read some of the authors I used to admire, I am appalled and more often than not put the book away. I recently turned with some trepidation to the new work by Anne Tyler, *Back when we were Old.* She writes so gracefully, I decided it was worth it to read her. What a lovely book. Not a single objectionable word or situation, and a fine read. I would almost guess that the Holy Spirit lives in her as well.

I confess I still watch the Comedy Channel, despite the raunchy language. And while I'm glad that George Bush is president, I didn't vote for him. There are vestiges of my earlier, sectarian life. But I'm sincerely trying to be "in the world but not of it." The handsome and Christian financial planner who manages my meager IRA is convinced this book will be a best seller and he will have lots of business from this senior. Not likely, but that reminds me of a story.

"When you are retired, what will you do? Your capital doesn't permit much of a fixed income." Those were the words of an Orlando financier. I got to thinking about that. Retire? I don't think I will. Fixed income? Who fixed it? One of the more challenging of the AA promises on page 83 of the book Alcoholics Anonymous is, "Fear of people and of financial insecurity will no longer bother us." God helps a lot with that. Security is an inside job, and my God is inside.

While we're musing about authority and the Holy Spirit giving companionship, I have to add that this last year I have really enjoyed my own company, and I guess that is another Holy Spirit consequence.(My spiritual advisor directed me to 1 Timothy 6: 1, where the subject of contentment is dealt with.) After church on Saturday I take myself out to dinner and have a little party with myself. When my husband died, I thought I would be really lonely but I'm not. I have friends and invite them in and there is always someone to go and do with. Ellie likes to go to the casinos and play the nickel machines and I do too! Geri gets up a car full to go to a spa. The Bunco ladies invite me to fill in. I love to be by myself and read and listen to music. And five of my grandchildren, last but not least, live 100 feet away. In addition, I'm flying to Orlando this week to see dear long-term friends. When I moved away from there a year ago to go to California, I vowed I would not lose track as I had done with my Boston friends. True to my word, I'm going to Orlando about twice a year. And God has shown me a way to do that. I have a Delta Sky Miles credit card, which builds up free trips, even though I pay it off at the end of each month. My phone, my satellite, my groceries, my gas, etc. etc. are just the expenses of daily living, but charged on the card they add up. I switch phone companies and car rental agencies at the drop of incentive 5000 miles and I upgrade to first class for $80. What a deal.

Chapter XIV

Brand Loyalty

A harbinger of a life to come took place in Boston in 1958. Three of my friends from the University of Kansas were studying at Harvard Business School. All of them went on to have distinguished careers, but that isn't the point. The point is, they gathered up all the recent KU grads they knew in the area and had a market study, one of the first in the nation. I was there, along with a group of other sorority gals (the fellows were Phi Delts, and we had dated them in days gone by) and I produced the most atypical market survey results ever gleaned.

The product at the time was a cleaner in a muscle-man shaped bottle called Mr. Clean. Recently resurrected, he is familiar today. We were asked if we used liquid household cleansers, a relatively new idea at the time, and eventually we got around to the brands. One of the gals said she liked to grab Mr. Clean by the waist and squeeze him. Most agreed. I demurred. "If there is a coupon for Mr. Clean, I'll buy it. Otherwise, I buy what there is a coupon for, whether its BAB-O or Spic and Span".

For years, I demonstrated no brand loyalty toward religion. I was a Presbyterian, an Episcopalian, a Religious Scientist, a member of Unity, and an Evangelical Christian. At the last-mentioned I cashed in my coupon for salvation.

Northland Church offered a product I really wanted: a huge, many faceted , Bible believing church with an energetic and appealing teacher-minister. When I moved to California and I found the same qualities in North Coast church, I signed on. What a fortunate soul I am to have found a religious home. I daily hear people say "I don't relate to organized religion," and I want to grab them and bring them to North Coast. Whether giving away sodas at events or ministering to young people or feeding the homeless or reckreating (my Mother's word which meant 'entertaining") seniors, the church has made me, in the pastor's words, a "Raving Fan."

Emmett Fox, a New Thought preacher of note in this century (he used to fill Madison Square Garden on Sundays) once observed that when troubled, we should think about God. "We can't entertain two thoughts at the same time" was his rationale. He called this principle his "Golden Key" and I have often employed it to my benefit. But I have a veritable tool box of remedies to being troubled, today. I call someone in my Growth Group. I pray, of course. I read my Bible. I turn on the radio to a Christian station and listen to praise music or a Christian message. I haul out my laptop, hook it up, and listen to a message on the internet. I have already detailed Raul Reis' site; how about Billy Graham's which is hourofdecision.org, or Gary Kusinake's site which is CCRSM.org or a million others all over the country. My own church is northcoastchurch.org and like the others, the sermon is recorded and posted and can be played on the computer. Ditto my former church, Northlandcc.net. Think of the veritable arsenal we have at our fingertips! And we don't even need a coupon. They're free. And all of them are worth it.

Brand loyalty doesn't have anything to do with it! God does.

Chapter XV

Abundant Life

"I have come that you might have life, and have it more abundantly." Jesus said that, and for years I thought that meant I was supposed to have lots of money. (That was BHS, or Before the Holy Spirit.) My first husband, who got pretty tired of living with a drunk, coughed up buckets of alimony to get rid of me, and I put that toward a really beautiful house which my second (but impecunious) husband then built. It was post and beam and fronted on a pond with a 20-acre hunk of swamp. We had total privacy, and often sunned au natural. The order, beauty, and symmetry of our home were widely admired, and friends asked to visit and almost always took pictures.

That was the kind of abundance I understood. I had always had a beautiful place to live. The home I grew up in in Pittsburg Kansas was a modified Victorian with wonderful, big rooms and a turret which was my study when I was young. My home in Belmont, Mass was a showplace with a greenhouse and a hillside garden and a view of Tufts University. Then came the home in Oviedo. Then came the Holy Spirit. Then came the inner conviction that I was not "where I lived."

Suddenly, abundance meant abundance of time to do what I loved: write, swim, entertain my friends one at a time, and travel.

In the End, It's Faith

I'm pretty sure that Jesus is pleased with my donations to the church and my gifts toward my grandchildren and my work for AA and my books which now center on the Kingdom. And my church work, which includes singing and setting up for services and a Growth Group. I count all these things as abundance, now. I am all but released from housework and home maintenance since I live in a tiny 5th Wheel which cleans up in half an hour. I have touches of abundance all through it in my sound system, my satellite, my ionizer, and my mink pillow and throw. (So it's mock mink. It certainly classes up the place.) That's about all the material abundance I covet.

Spiritual abundance is what I have now. I can pray, meditate, listen to Calvary radio and praise music, and feast my eyes on the absolutely breathtaking view of canyons, valleys, and mountains from my deck, and drive to the ocean in 20 minutes. That's the real McCoy.

This modest effort, which grows abundantly from chapter to chapter, will have to be put on hold for a time as I go to Orlando next week to celebrate with my AA friends their 30th and 40th birthdays of sobriety, then hop a plane for Greensboro to see grandchildren. Everything I want, I have today. A loving family. Loving friends.Leisure. God is indeed, good. AHS (After the Holy Spirit) I'm quite content.

Chapter XVI

God, Cats, and Chocolate Cake

After I emigrated from Florida to North Coast Church in California, I signed on to mind the Kindergartners while their mothers were in Bible study. While I eventually had to relinquish the post due to the little ones wanting me to join them on the floor (and then I couldn't get back up) I loved the job the year I did it.

These sweethearts were ready for the Kingdom of Heaven, all right. In that year, one of the dearest said her father had taken his computer and left for good, but she smiled up at me and said "But like Jesus, he'll always be in my heart." Another was tearful one day because she worried that when she went to heaven she couldn't take her dog. A third chimed in, wanting to know if God was a cat person or a dog person. That one was easy. Both. God even loves sparrows.

In general, we asked them to direct the weightiest questions or worries to their parents. I was keenly aware that I was no authority. But if a quick check with a mommy in a week or two divulged that they hadn't, I would relay the concern.

And often, like the sparrows instance, the answer came right out of scripture. One Sunday I baked the treat, a chocolate cake. The mothers, queried before the session, gave their approval. But one hesitant four-year-old, at snack time, wasn't so sure she should have it. "Is it OK with God to have cake in his house?" queried Gwen. We asked her how she felt about Chocolate cake. With some enthusiasm, she answered "I love it." Well, then, we said, Jesus said that he loves you and wants to give you the desires of your heart, and that includes Chocolate cake.

Every week we did a Bible study of our very own. While the mothers were in the Video Café listening to a lecturer, their children were in our classroom playing with playdough Daniels and Goliaths after reading the book and coloring in a line drawing of the conflict. After games and snacks, they watched a video of David and Goliath, animated of course, and that rather cemented the story. When we asked them if they remembered the story and could tell it a week later, the answers were "certainly," and they did just that. A wonderful Child Care Supervisor planned the lessons and when we reported for duty at 9 a.m. we had all our supplies, even the video laid out on the teacher's table. That made it even easier to concentrate on the children.

At playtime, we had a store with all kinds of make-believe products for sale, from fresh fish to toys. The family corner included a crib and a stove and sink and lots of "babies" who were sung to and put to bed. There were usually 9 or so four-year-olds and they got along remarkably well. It was sheer pleasure to be "Miss Letty" to them, and I miss them to this day. Fortunately, my daughter and her husband after producing three teens of their own adopted an African-American two year old and his brother, four months. Caleb, the older one, is pushing three and has all the wonder and excitement that that age encourages. When I tell him about David and Goliath and that it's a story God told, he sings "God is Bigger" from Veggie Tales. Like my old class of dear ones, he knows about God. And now, instead of "Miss Letty," I'm Grandma. How very lovely.

Chapter XVII

Watching the Superbowl

When I read my grandfather's journal about coming as a boy to Missouri from Pennsylvania in wagons, I am absolutely astonished that today I can be in Orlando for a party, in Greensboro N.C. for a visit, and in California the next night in my very own bed. In fewer than 200 years, we have racheted up our efficiency beyond my grandfather's wildest dreams. Compare the pony express, where letters took weeks to be delivered, to email.

A dear friend sent me a book some years ago in which he pointed out that we were older than television, than polio vaccine, than the Brooklyn bridge, than zircons, and a whole raft of such new-fangled stuff. The list has grown exponentially.(I may be older than that word....)

My first husband was an MIT professor; in the 50's he took me to see the MIT computer which lived in a huge air conditioned room. I realize now that it had to be cooled because of the heat from the vacuum tubes! The computer was easily 75 feet long and the size of the pool I do laps in at my health club. Today, that same computational ability rests in this tiny laptop at my fingertips. In the movie Peggy Sue Gets Married, the heroine is a time traveler and tells a friend in High School that "in the future, everything gets smaller except for radios which get larger." I now have a logpad and a telephone which compute as well.

And giving the lie to Peggy Sue, I have a tiny radio.

My grandfather gave me his Bible. It, characteristically, is huge with births and deaths and marriages listed on the title page. It is, of course, the King James translation. That was the whole ball game then. Now we have so many translations we have to cite two or three for each reference, it seems. In my growth group at North Coast, Earl has The Way translation and I have the NIV and so does Emma and etc. Since there is now even a politically correct translation, the mind boggles. Someday, growth group members, each with their own Bible translation, will spend a whole day parsing one verse......(I would think I had the gift of prophecy, except in college, I wrote that Rock and Roll will never last.)

The Superbowl, this year, between Oakland and Tampa Bay, was deeply satisfying. Tampa, the underdog, won in a walk, and the spectators sat in the very seats I had frequented in San Diego. Since I have spent 23 years in Florida and one in California, Tampa was my team. I watched the game from my daughter's lovely home in Greensboro, after the grandsons had packed it in.

Something about Americans, they love heroic contests, and the SB was one such. I suspect we are mirroring the contest between the forces of light and the forces of darkness, but the teams we root for are not so cut and dried. Plenty of folks out there are cheering for the worldly team: getting their "stuff." Dedicated materialists as I once was, they can't see the virtue of another point of view. Even sometimes, the spiritual life is mocked and derided.

There is a concept that all roads lead to the same God. I am guilty of writing that in an earlier book. It just isn't true. My God offers salvation through grace, not works or detachment as the other major religions do. God gave Jesus to atone for my sins, thus offering me a ticket to a heavenly Superbowl where the good guys always win..

And like my MIT computer and my grandfather's Bible, the Heavenly stadium is enormous. And the only thing you give up to get in is your pride when you ask for forgiveness of your sins. Then, Jesus gives you a pass for eternity. . "He has made everything beautiful in its time. He has set eternity in the hearts of men..."NIV Ecclesiastes 3:11

Chapter XVIII

What Do God and Fog Have in Common?

Back on California soil and home in my tiny trailer, I look out an otherwise stunning vista to a wall of fog. For 23 years a Floridian, and a swamp dweller at that, I thought fog was indigenous to that part of the world. Since I wasn't a believer for most of that time, I didn't try to fathom God's works there. My husband, also not a believer, was so enamored of the setting that more religious people saluted his nearness to a creator. One example of that was the Episcopal Bishop's wife who called to pray when he had his first heart attack.

Since I have encountered fog in such diverse places as West Virginia and Guatemala, in Lisbon and in Malta, then I can find the first of a number of comparisons between God and fog. They're omnipresent. They have no geographical center.

The second similarity is that they both surprise us. Author and Seminary head James Dobson writes that God loves surprises, and the weatherman here is more often wrong than right when fog is predicted. One of the most famous, and deservedly so, Christian books was written by Cambridge Don C. S..Lewis who, at his conversion, was "Surprised by Joy." Since I never plan what to do about events or people, but simply do my best and leave the results up to God, then I am continually surprised.

Currently, my daughter and her husband are separated in North Carolina, and since both of them are dedicated parents, they each have their four boys on alternate weeks. As a consequence, Bill has learned pretty much what it means to be a mother. Carole has a job, bringing in income, and she's learned about the tensions of being a breadwinner. Their icy relationship is thawing, and God really shocked me with this one. My prediction was that the separation would simply lead to more bitterness. In a word, their fog is lifting.

But the greatest similarity is that the fog is lifting here, and in minutes I have to set out for Carlsbad and my growth group. Just as God has revealed more and more to me about worship, the Christian life, his Word, and his love, so do I see glimpses of the heretofore beautiful landscape out my window. And the mist is rolling heavenward. Soon, the way will be clear. NIV 2 Corinthians 12:2-4 Paul is speaking about a beating that almost led to his death and says "I know a man in Christ who 14 years ago was caught up in the third heaven...and I know that man was caught up to paradise. He heard inexpressible things; I do not know but God knows."Always a good thing to remember.

Chapter XIX

Mansions and Butlers

Late last night I got an East Coast phone call from a friend who filled me in on her latest crisis. After deaths, abandonments, financial reverses, lawsuits, and a litany of horrors I could only marvel at, she had not lost her faith. A long-time believer, she insisted that God meant it for good, as the scripture says. Without thinking, I told her that "in my father's house are many mansions, and you get the one with the butler."

Then lo and behold this morning I got Bruce Wilkinson's new book, *A Life God Rewards"* which lays out the very same premise. He says our life on earth is rewarded in heaven, a belief I have ascribed to for years. I wrote about it in my last book, *Turn Your Eyes.* It's why, for example, I wrote that book: to utilize my writing skills for the Lord. Wilkinson's turn on the subject includes formulating the Law of the Unbreakable Link: choices on earth have direct consequences on your life in eternity. Surely, with all her steadfastness in the face of travail, Elaine will get a bevy of servants, not just a butler.

Over and over in the Bible is the point driven home that we are saved by Grace, not by works. But the works have to count for something. There are endless jokes about the clergy and the various professions and how their lives are treated differently once they get to heaven, from roller skates to Mercedes to travel in and luxurious homes versus shacks to live in. Just as Paul told us that our hearts are hid in eternity, man has an intuitive grasp of the fact that eternity will be different for each inhabitant. The story of the Rich Man and Lazarus in the Word sets that out for all to read.

Ideally, with my eyes on the prize which is eternity, I will choose differently every minute of my life. I had a querulous moment this morning with an American Express customer service rep, and immediately apologized. I saw a giant blackboard with my name and a black mark being forgiven by a scorekeeping Jesus. That is probably carrying this idea a bit too far, but as my brother says, " Nothing succeeds like excess." Uppermost in my mind is that I want to live a life acceptable to God. I'm even going for "pleasing," these days

Well, then, what rewards can I expect for the effort of writing? As I told Elaine this morning, I'm just hoping for a really good mattress and a berth in the alto section of the Heavenly choir. Is that too much to ask?

Chapter XX

Built-Ins

My late husband was a skilled carpenter. He designed and built entertainment centers, bars, even beds and dressing tables and mailboxes. He almost always fashioned a secret drawer in whatever he was building, to the delight of the buyer. He called them his "built-ins".

As I grow older, a little wiser, and observe more and more people, I think our heavenly Father has made us with "built-ins", too. Even before the Holy Spirit joins us in living a purposeful life, almost everyone has the desire to minister. In disasters, the most common response is to pitch in and help. Teachers and social workers, helping professions, do their work despite low pay and sometimes really awful working conditions. They want to help, too. "Christianity Today" has an article this month about the rise of new organizations which plan a New Paradigm of business, where businessmen are taught that they will lead the way in making Americans a new sensitive, loving people. They, like the teachers, social workers, and preachers, are being given a mission.

I first noticed this phenomenon and wrote about it in a previous book. A good friend became president of his Homeowner's Association and used the post to bring a gentler, kinder outlook to his members. Because of his loving spirit, the small association became more purposeful and cooperative, and that was his goal.

Most every little boy and girl think they'll grow up to be president. Why? To fix things. To help the country. That would seem to be the motive, as well, for those who give up lucrative posts in industry to join the president's cabinet. (Some may be power-grabbers, it's true, but there is initial altruism, as well.)

The most satisfying part, for me, of 25 years in Alcoholics Anonymous is the time I have spent sponsoring women in the program, taking them through the 12 Steps, and advising them about living a sober life. In other words, helping them. And more and more senior people in organizations get their major kick out of "mentoring" others.

Although we have a sinful nature, we have patches of built in divinity. Author Wayne Dyer writes that if we squeeze an orange, we get orange juice. If pressure leads to altruism when pressure squeezes an individual, surely it's because God put the altruism there. Because our better instincts are God-inspired, we follow them to our glory and ignore them to our peril. Have you ever made a decision to do something knowing that you shouldn't? I have. That "knowing" is a God thing. The Holy Spirit convicts us that we are on shaky ground when we sin. Even the apostle Paul wrote that he did things he didn't want to do and didn't do things he knew he should.

A newly-sober man in his initial month of AA said one day with surprise: "It feels good to do the right thing." As psychologist B.F. Skinner divined, reinforcement, or positive acknowledgement of an act (feeling good) makes that act stronger. My AA friend was heading Godward. As I progress in my spirit, I pray that I am, too.

Chapter XXI

Reading and Listening
and Grandma Moses

I just listened to a program on the Calvary Broadcast Network, Mike Macintosh of Harvest Fellowship, and I thought to myself "he has years and years of Bible exposition to his credit and has forgotten more about Jesus than I'll ever know and why on earth would anyone consider reading what unschooled I have to say?

I ran that uncertainty by my spiritual advisor who reminded me that it's hard to listen to the radio on an airplane and that programs aren't as available as a book; sometimes I have to wait a whole week to listen to someone I admire. Besides, if I need to fill in some down time (at the laundry, at the checkout) it's great to have a little tome to peruse. (I love my spiritual advisor). I guess I do have a place in the scheme of things.

Once the self-help author Alan Cohen observed in one of his books that he had no idea that so many self-help books had been written when he wrote his first. "Had I known, I probably wouldn't have written this book; I would have been too intimidated," he said. I'm exactly that way with Christian books. Until I found a Christian bookstore, I assumed that the total of the genre could be found in four shelves at Borders. How wrong I was. Just the other day I offered to fill in at a conference for a friend who didn't want to cancel a conflicting golf game. "You don't know anything about it," he said scornfully, and I pointed out that had never stopped me before.

As I may have stated and restated, I am a new Christian, a baby in Christ, and I've only got two and a half years under my belt of living AHS, or after the Holy Spirit. Just as I'm sure I'm rendered unfit to write, I get compared to my new adopted grandson, who is two and a half. He has learned to walk and to run and to throw a ball and to swing and to climb after being a little blob of smiles like his brother, Nate. Caleb has also learned to talk, to do his numbers, to obey, to hug, to kiss, to work the television; his repertoire is magnificent. I hope I've applied myself as diligently to growing in Christ as Caleb has to growing up .Anyhow, he makes me see what is possible in a few short years and encourages me to study harder. I guess I'm stirred along by the number of birthdays under my belt; I don't have a lot of years left to be as knowledgeable as Mike Macintosh or Tony Campolo or Philip Yancey or any other of my heroes. My spiritual advisor says I can write a "primitive" book that's beautiful, just as famous painter Grandma Moses could paint a beautiful primitive painting. Sometimes, schooling dampens down the heart.

Chapter XXII

Living Examples

Of course, I can't even write the first syllable of this chapter without thinking of Jesus, the ultimate Living Example. That was the perfect Godly life. But my original focus was something closer to home.

Whenever I have had to advise some junior person, whether in my college sorority as a pledge mother or as a sponsor in the AA program or even as an officer in a group with a board member, doing so has raised my standards. Let me explain: I can't, in good conscience, tell a new member of AA to go to many many meetings without having done so myself. If I do not go, I am a hollow advisor likely to be ignored. If I do attend several meetings, I am better off and my sobriety is strengthened, even after many years of not drinking.

And if I tell a new Christian how grand my life is with Christ and then I carp and complain, I won't be believable. Hence, I don't focus on the negative. That's one place where the new consciousness people are right. If I believe, as the Bible says, that all things work together for good for those who love God and are called according to his purposes, then negativity has no place in my life. There is no such thing. There is just my limited perspective. When Joseph's brothers sold him as a slave to Egyptians, anyone would think it terrible, but because of this he saved his brothers from famine when he was Prime Minister of Egypt, again after reversals and "terrible " events that turned out to fulfill God's plan. That simple example has raised my own attitudes many times. When my husband died suddenly, when my house burned down, I knew that God meant it for good. Of course, I didn't know that right away, and for a time I felt devastated. But I know that in the long run, perhaps in eternity, I'll get it.

I often wonder if being a pastor has this same result: being more Godly because he preaches Godliness to others.

There are occasionally striking examples of this trust being breeched, but these exceptions probably prove the rule.

Actually, this living example rule should encourage others to take leadership roles in their church or other organization, because they stand the chance of improving their performance as well. Like Avis, I try harder when I'm telling someone what to do.

Chapter XXIII

Swimming for the Greater Glory

The prophet Isaiah, writing of the coming of the kingdom of heaven, says (25:11) "They will spread out their hands in it as a swimmer spreads out his hands to swim. God will bring down their pride, despite the cleverness (uncertainty) of their hands." Do you know why I cite that? Because I just got out of the swimming pool, and sure enough I spread out my hands and God brought down my pride. I had another one of those "I don't have anything to say" days. My angel, usually so accommodating when I sit down at the computer, evidently had better things to do than inspire me. But yesterday I told my writing class at the Adult Center that considering writing as a job meant working it up high on my list of priorities, and doing it all the time.

Hoist by my own petard. As I noted above, when I give advice to others I'd better follow it myself. I can write that God is exceedingly near when I'm swimming. I have tried walking meditation in a class and had glimpses of what that does, but God and meditation when I swim are nearer. I can, of course, get into a rhythm and swim without thinking, just chug back and forth in my laps and get into an endorphin high. Sounds secular, doesn't it? But who put those endorphins there? Not me. God, read Jesus, is my creator. I think God lives in endorphins.

In the End, It's Faith

The cabinet in my kitchen that frequently whacks me in the shins yesterday crunched my shoeless big toe and at first, swimming hurt. After a while, it felt so good to be in the rhythm of the swim that I forgot about my toe. That's a God thing, too. The apostle Paul wrote of an unspecified ailment, a "thorn in the flesh" which he had prayed to have removed, to no avail. I had forgotten to pray about the pain in my toe but my amazing God fixed it, anyway. Why would God treat me better than his greatest missionary? That's one of those things that Pastor Larry talked about last night at church. He said that God rewards us all, we all get a great deal when our sins are forgiven and we are promised eternity by accepting Christ. But some in the kingdom get greater rewards than others, and he used the illustration of grace by telling the parable in Matthew 25 of the vineyard. In that story, the owner hires workers all day long and pays those who came last as much as those who had been there since morning. Larry said we mustn't, like the workers, lose sight of the fact that we had an enormous gift from God because some are more rewarded than others.

I took myself out for prime rib after church and thought how I was really much more fortunate than most of the people I knew, by my lights. There are those who would look at my life and not think that, but I count myself the luckiest person alive. In 1978 I joined my health club because it had a swimming pool. Then I moved and the pool in the club here is better. Just one more of God's blessings. Like a swimmer, I'm reaching out my hands....

Chapter XXIV

I am the Alpha, and the Omega

In my Unitarian Church in Belmont, Mass, my choir director's name was Alpha. I considered her musical taste impeccable, and her guidance one of the great assets of the church. I didn't think that highly of the minister, whom I had voted against when he came to our church for a trial sermon. (Nobody else shared my opinion, then, so he was selected. Later, he was given an ultimatum to stop an unproductive habit or step down. Lots of disenchantment reigned at that time.) I had studied Greek, and when our first puppy was selected, we named him Alpha, too. It seemed to be a unisex name. My volunteer activity at the time was to be the advisor for my college sorority's alpha chapter at Boston University. There were, in the 1960's lots of "firsts", as my first of three daughters had been born, the first book I had written was finished, the first house we owned was purchased, my first commitment to a mental hospital was undertaken, and my first marriage began to fall apart.

Omega was the name of the second, and last dog. My husband and I were divorced, I left for Florida and a job, and Omega stayed with a loving family in Boston. Between Alpha and Omega, an awful lot of water went over the dam. The three daughters scattered to opposite coasts, places they still live. But they all came to Florida for my second husband's funeral, a real "omega" occasion. Their presence mitigated what would otherwise have been an awful ending to Dan's and my life together. He had died suddenly on Easter Sunday of a heart attack and could not be revived by the EMT personnel who came swiftly when I called 911.

Later, I went to Maine to visit my youngest daughter and while I was there the house, which Dan had lovingly designed and built with his own hands, burned. Another ending, another Omega.

I was not a believer then, but my two youngest daughters were and they both witnessed to me telling me that Christ could be a balm to my devastation. They were praying for me, and their friends and churches were praying for me. Later, through a series of circumstances after being saved I met several of their friends who had prayed for my salvation, and one of them is now my spiritual advisor.

My oldest daughter is the object of much prayer from all three of our churches today, as she faces a separation from her husband which could end in divorce and disruption for their four sons. I am heartsick at the prospect, but I know the situation will evolve as God wants it to. I can't help but hope, however, that this is not another ending but the beginning of a stronger union for both of them.

Jesus said "I am the alpha and the omega" That means to me he is there for my beginnings and for my endings, and for the beginnings and endings of all believers. A church I visited while looking for a church home has the Greek letters Alpha and Omega on its podium. I did not elect to stay there, but I loved the reminder. Just as that altar promised, Jesus is everything.

Chapter XXV

The Glad Guy

In Hebrews is the statement that Jesus was the gladdest guy (anointed with the oil of gladness above all his fellows 1:9) He was also the prince of sorrows, but in those instances it was for other people, not himself. That's why fishermen and tax collectors left their tasks behind and followed him. That's why he was able to attract multitudes, have his feet washed with precious oil, and be welcomed by hospitality from even Pharisees who wanted, really, to kill him. He must have been a great fellow to have around.

Do you know anyone in your circle who is like that? Always positive? Always jolly? Always sensitive? I don't. That is why Jesus was unique, one of a kind. He never sinned, he never transgressed, he was a perfect man, and one with a winning personality.

The question, "what would Jesus do?" today is hardly ever answered "He would laugh." But he would. He would relish the funny and get a huge kick out of some jokes that come over the internet. When he thought of his father in heaven, he called him "Abba," or daddy. In his times of solitude, I'll bet he regaled his father with stories of that regenerate Peter or the loving John, and they laughed together. "Did you see Peter's face when he stepped out on the water, looked away, and began to sink? Wasn't that some expression?" "What do you think of that Martha being peeved when Mary talked to me instead of helping her in the kitchen?" (chuckle, chuckle.) When Jesus talked things over with his father, they undoubtedly shared many a laugh at the foibles of the individuals who followed Jesus. After all, the father knew what Jesus knew, and that makes a perfect companion to talk things over with.

As I matured, I grew closer to my mother. We had fun talking to each other about situations and events and we often did that. As my daughters mature, I have fun talking to them. I love them, so I delight in them. I did when they were younger, too, but now we're equals and it's better.

I betcha the father delighted in Jesus. He loved him and was proud enough to say on the Mount of Transfiguration, "This is my son (Matthew 17:5, Matthew 3:16,17) and to laud him at his baptism with the Holy Spirit. The father was a proud Abba, and he had lots to be proud of. The lame walked, the blind saw, the lepers were cleansed, demons were cast out, and Jesus chose to give his life for us and reconcile God to us sinners. He was perfect, and he was amazing. And, except for his travail in the Garden of Gethsemene, his fury with the money changers in the temple, and his time upon the cross, he was anointed with gladness. May we be the same.

Chapter XXVI

Spirit or World?

Occasionally, we're faced with choices so difficult that we just leave them up to God. This morning brought such a choice for me. At 7 a.m. Pacific time I could watch U.S. Secretary of State Colin Powell on the dissimulation by Iraq about its weapons of mass destruction, or I could listen to Rev. Chuck Smith's program on KWVE, the station he founded along with the Calvary Network in the '80's. After a little "which" struggle, I opted for Chuck Smith because I knew I could read about Powell's speech in the paper. A few minutes into a discussion of Deuteronomy, I knew I had heard this lesson before, that it was a repeat of a Smith broadcast of some months ago. Back to Powell and the United Nations. God had solved that dilemma for me as he does on so many occasions.

Only a few of my acquaintance had faced that struggle, I learned, when I got to my Growth Group. As we do, we answered questions about Sunday's sermon, mentioned above, but first we shared about Colin Powell and war. Reluctantly, we came to the same conclusion: He had made the case for engagement with the Iraqis based on the U.N resolution that they must cooperate with inspectors or be disarmed. The price of "Peace at any Price" had risen too high.

It was a blessing to turn our attention to the scriptures, and our leaders, Carol and Tom, shared with us.

"Don't confuse the gifts of the Holy Spirit with talents," said Carol after our discussion of the talents given the servants in Matthew 25.(The story is, a departing master gives his wealth to his servants; two double the amount, one hides it in the ground "from fear it will be lost.") Larry, our pastor, pointed out in the sermon that "talents" is not only a word for money but also for abilities, which is the point of Jesus' parable.) Carol said that talents are abilities, like musical ability or intelligence that we are more or less born with, but that compassion, gentleness, and self control, for example, are gifts that can come to us through accepting the Holy Spirit into our lives.

We were asked how we were spending our talents and gifts to advance the Kingdom. Some kindly enough mentioned my book, *Turn Your Eyes,* and Marydale lauded Ann's caring, nurturing manner toward the nursing home patients we sing to in the Over 55 Singers. Marydale's organizing ability and piano playing talents are very much a part of that as well, we said. Like the last two mentioned, many believers don't see the great services they are performing in the world; they take their actions as a matter of course. Tom said he hoped God would say "Well done, good and faithful servant," when he got to heaven. That was the greatest reward he could imagine. I'm pretty sure that is highly likely to happen. For all of us.

The Recliner

"I hate to buy something from a fellow Christian, because we both want diametrically opposite results. I want the lowest price for the object, and she wants the highest price." My daughter Nancy smiled ruefully, and said "besides, she's a darling woman with a little baby. I really want to help her."

The object in question was a recliner, advertised in the Fallbrook (CA) weekly newspaper. Nancy had searched the internet, had gone to several stores, and knew the selection she wanted: a leather recliner, either reconditioned or new. Laurie had it, and it massaged and vibrated as well. Since my son-in-law performs hundreds of favors for me a month, including taking out my trash, I wanted to chip in for the recliner because it was his birthday present. My initial choice was a beige new recliner at the Salvation Army which had two soil marks on the rear, the side toward the wall. The cost was $89, and I would have been ecstatic with it if it were my recliner. The combination of something really comfortable and good looking plus the fact that it was a bargain made it for me, irresistible.

But Nancy wanted to spoil Jamie. "He has his heart set on a leather one," she told me. A lovely reconditioned one was being sold on eBay for $1200. That was a long way from $89! Then came the newspaper ad.

"She wanted almost as much as eBay" Nancy said, but then Laurie offered a compromise figure when Nancy cited the eBay price. The vibrating, massaging, leather, two month old recliner was within reach, but Nancy told her she wasn't going to do it right away, but was going to pray about it. I okayed the price from my half, and since it was a deluxe chair for Jamie's office, where clients could someday come, and it was what he really wanted, it was brought home to surprise him after a trip had taken him out of town.

Nancy and I got to sit in it first. And it truly was a thing of beauty, and a focal point for the office. I decided, somewhat reluctantly, that it was, indeed, a better buy than the Salvation Army recliner. That was primarily because it was what Jamie wanted.

"What one of you who asks his father for bread will be given a stone? (Matthew 7:9 How much more will your father in heaven give good gifts....) Jamie is a great husband and an amazing father, and a devoted son in law. For him, I want to go the second mile. For him, I want to do my best to give him the desires of his heart. Jamie once said of a mutual acquaintance, "he has a heart for God." Well, it takes one to know one. Additionally, I often ask him if I am a good enough Mother in Law. I suspect God wants me to be one, for sure .Is the recliner some kind of evidence????

Chapter XXVIII

Christian Books

Every now and then—and sometimes weekly—something comes along that fills me with humility. The latest lesson is a statistic. On a web site, I read that 100,000 Christian books were published last year. Since mine was one of them, and I had been feeling rather grand about it, the sheer number of my peers overwhelmed me. Now, you have read of my feeling that no one would want to hear what I have to say, and I do feel that way, sometimes. But one of 100,000? That is a pretty humbling number. Now I'm even more doubtful that anyone will read *"Turn Your Eyes"*. Or, *"In the End It's Faith"*. I can only hope that my children and grandchildren will read them and be, therefore, the bulk of my audience.

I have 11 grandchildren and three daughters and their husbands, plus varied church members of mine who have been generous with their orders for the book and I guess that will have to be a beginning.

Now, the question arises is the Holy Spirit out convicting all these 100,000-plus authors to write, and do they all depend, as I do, on the Holy Spirit to convince friends and children and grandchildren to read? I know when I read the Bible as literature for a college course that it didn't mean much to me. When I read it as a person investigating Christianity it didn't mean much to me. When I accepted Jesus into my life and was prompted by the Holy Spirit, I thought the Bible was wonderful. I couldn't read it enough; I wanted more. I also wanted to read about the Christian life and Christian thought. I couldn't get enough of that, either. It was an older, wiser Christian who advised me to concentrate on the Word, and not get lost in theology or Christology or that impressive word, hermeneutics.

He said, "read the word. Phillip Yancey has his interpretation and Max Lucado has his interpretation and you want to get one of your own God speaks to you, too." I wonder if he ever regrets his having set in motion my own interpretation. But I know he's right: God speaks to me individually, and I know he does it through his Word. I can see better when I'm inspired, and James said in 1:17 that whatever is good and perfect comes from God.

God not only wants me to live to please him, he wants me to use whatever gifts I have to serve him. That's my justification for writing every day, and trying to tap into the Holy Spirit's inspiration. I suspect all 99,999 other authors are doing the same. We're all striving for the good and perfect article, the good and perfect book, even the good and perfect sentence. And I'll bet many of their number are as humbled by the statistics and I am. And I certainly hope all of them have as many grandchildren as I do. And relatives. And church friends. And, for the pastors (for they write the bulk of the books) parishioners with the means to buy books. The audience is spread thin, sure enough.

Chapter XXIX

Heavenly Customer Service

First Voice: "Yes, this is God's customer service department. I'm the angel Gabriel. How may I help you?"

Second Voice: "This is King Saul. I need God's help to catch and kill David."

First Voice: "I know something about that. God doesn't want you to catch and kill David. God has great plans for David, who is a man after his own heart."

Second Voice: "But I am anointed of God. I am the King, the one Samuel chose when the people wanted a ruler rather than a judge. A man who was the handsomest and tallest in the land. Why does God frustrate me?"

First Voice: There is another way to look at that. Why do you frustrate yourself? When did you pray, last? Why have you fallen into sin? Why do you seek to murder? Why didn't you follow God's directions when you conquered enemy people? Why do you covet? God hates that."

Second Voice: I don't want a lecture. I want God to help me."

First Voice: "You want God to help you with an evil plan. He won't. God is just."

Second Voice: "Then I'll get David without him…..(hangs up)"

Well, that's how it would have gone if God had a Customer Service department. But, of course, he doesn't need one. Impossible as it sounds, he handles everything himself and does it perfectly. As director of the universe, he is second to none. And you know how the conflict came out. David has opportunities to kill Saul but spares him, and Saul goes off to battle, is killed, and David becomes king. That skips all the symbolism and other metaphor, and all the life lessons, but that sums it all up.

For the full story, read your Bible. First Samuel would be a good place to start, but don't stop there. We've just scratched the surface of the good stuff.

Chapter XXX

Worry? What Me Worry?

Exodus 14, verses 13 and 14 show Moses responding to the people's lament that it would have been better for them to be slaves in Egypt rather than be killed by the pursuing army. "Do not be afraid. (Do not worry.) Stand firm, and you will see the deliverance the Lord will bring you. The Egyptians you see today you will never see again….."

Last night at church, we were all asked by guest pastor Gary Oliver how many of us had worried during the past week. Almost every hand went up. The country, after all, is facing war, a moribund economy with a loss of retirement income for elders, and a state budget that will have to cut many needed services. We were ripe for worry. He guided us to Numbers 13:25-26 Those verses summarized the report of the Israeli spies who went into the promised land, and 10 or the 12 reported it really wasn't possible to take the land as it was ruled by giants and soundly fortified.

Oliver traced their race into worry: Verse 28, the first stage of their worry, observation. Stage 2, verse 31, interpretation. Stage 3, verse 32, exaggeration, and Stage 4, Verse 33 "We seemed like grasshoppers in our own eyes and looked the same to them." "Worry happens," said Oliver. "Faith is a choice. We can choose to react with worry or respond with faith."

He sent us to Philippians 4:4-9 to find a remedy to worry. "Rejoice in the Lord, always," it reads, and tells the believer to present his petitions to God and God will reward him with the peace "that passes all understanding."

And here's the clincher: "Finally, brothers, whatever is pure, whatever is lovely, whatever is admirable, if anything is excellent or praiseworthy, think about such things. Whatever you have heard from me or seen in me, put it into practice and the God of peace will be with you."

In his enthusiastic way, Oliver read off a list of other verses that quell an anxious heart. Psalm 37, 1-9. It begins "do not fret because of evil men, or be envious of those who do wrong. For like the grass they will soon within, like green plants they will soon die away. Trust in the Lord and do good, dwell in the land and enjoy safe pasture. Delight yourself in the Lord, and he will give you the desires of your heart...."

Next, Psalm 40 verses 1-3: I waited patiently for the Lord; he turned to me and heard my cry. He lifted me out of the slimy pit, out of the mud and mire. He set my feet on a rock, and gave me a firm place to stand. He put a new song in my mouth, a hymn of praise to our God. Many will see and fear, and put their trust in the Lord. Proverbs 3, 5 and 6: Trust in the Lord with all your heart, and lean not on your own understanding. In all your ways acknowledge him, and he will make your paths straight...

Matthew 6:33 "But seek his kingdom and his righteousness, and all these things will be given to you. Therefore do not worry about tomorrow; for tomorrow will worry about itself, Each day has enough trouble of its own. Romans 8:28-29 And we know that in all things God works for the good of those who love him; who have been called according to his purpose. For those God foreknew he also predestined to be conformed to the likeness of his son, that he might be the firstborn among many brothers.

How about 1 Corinthians, 10:13? For no temptation has seized you that is not common to man And God is faithful. He will not let your be tempted beyond what you can bear. But when you are tempted, he will also provide a way out so you can stand up under it. Phillippians 1:6 Being confident of this, that he who began a good work in you will carry it on to completion until the day of Christ Jesus. Philippians 4: 13 I can do everything through him who gives me strength.1 Peter 5:10And   the God of all grace who called you to his eternal glory in Christ, after you have suffered a little while will himself restore you and make you strong, firm, and steadfast.

Said Pastor Oliver, worry robs us of precious time, magnifies our problems, makes up more impatient, can lead to physical and mental problems, and can even paralyze us when we need constructive action. He recommends putting each of the above verses on a card and reading them, out loud, to counter worry. I've made it easy for you: just reread this chapter.

Chapter XXXI

I Heard it on the Radio

President Bush speaks to the Association of Religious Broadcasters today, and that reminds me what an important role these folks play. In Orlando, Z88, which I sometimes listen to on my computer, was such a force for good for me that it aided in my conversion. I joined the two wonderful morning team members, Scott and Lisa, in prayer every morning and felt such a part of the Christian community. Z88 was light on teaching and was really a praise music station, a fact I became aware of when I moved to Vista CA and heard Chuck Smith's station, KWVE which featured teaching and preaching from Calvary Costa Mesa and other Calvary teachers in addition to a little praise music.

Z88 was listener supported, rather like a PBS station. KWVE is supported by ministers who buy time to present their messages, then appeal to their listeners for funds. That seems to be the most common form of religious station management. In November of 2002, the National Religious Broadcasters opened a headquarters building in Manassas, Va. "At last we have a home after 60 years," the press release read. Their spokesperson for their web site is probably one of their lobbyists, and they have willing ears in the

Bush administration. President Bush dedicated their new
building and is the keynoter at their convention in Nash-
ville this month (Feb 2003).

On their web site, which is NRB.org, I looked in vain
for statistics on how many listeners to Christian radio are
Christians, but a source at KWVE said more than 30 per
cent of the listeners to religious programs don't call themselves Christians, and are waiting to hear the Gospel. If
that figure is accurate, think of the impact these stations
have. There are 1600 members of the NRB located all over
the continent and reaching millions. Air1, a conglomerate
of such stations into a network, is a music ministry that we
tracked across the country when we drove from Florida to
California.

At the convention are "Boot Camps," or break-out teaching sessions on producing religious material from such
heavy hitters as Phil Cook who produced Planet of the Apes
and other mega-movies. Members can study up on how to
use the Internet, design web sites, how to handle Email,
and a program for listening to panels of Christian radio
consumers. Station owners and managers are also advised
on "Your Greatest Mistakes." Clearly, this event is a tremendous builder of bridges to the Christian radio
community.

And if you get the President as your keynoter, you're
not doing half badly.

Chapter XXXII

A Convergence, Briefly

I believe my lifetime was extended, today. How? I relaxed in Jamie's recliner, the expensive recliner, that massages back and calves and is wonderfully good to look at.

While I wouldn't have believed it, it's worth the money. But, you ask, what does that have to do with convergence? Well, I dialed up the Fox network and found President Bush's speech to the NRB while I vibrated. And two chapters of this effort came together. Earlier, I had listened to a CNN broadcast on Shock and Awe as a tactic in war, which involves getting an enemy so intimidated that he quits before a shot is fired. Devoutly, I wished that would happen. The chance that a single attack will lead to a world-wide attack is too great.

Between the reducing threat of war and the enormously relaxing effect of the recliner, I can almost forget to worry about a nuclear holocaust next month. Yes, another convergence. And believe me, I have been reading those verses in the chapter on worry over and over.

On Fox, Jaques Chicaq of France and Alexander Putin of Russia are sharing my fear of unintended consequences to military action. While Colin Powell was convincing that Sadam Hussein has to be disarmed, it is looking more and more like that might be possible without war. U2 flights are being accepted by Iraq, and more inspectors are being sent from France and Russia. It could be Sadam might indeed turn over his weapons of mass destruction.

As the Bible predicts, we will all, all over the world, be able to track the likelihood of wars and talks of wars. Thanks to CNN, Fox, CNBC, MSNBC.

How did we used to wait for the evening news and the morning paper to learn what was going on? Today, the very thought seems archaic.

Today, my mood can rise and fall with the next News Alert.

However, as long as I'm vibrating, it doesn't matter as much.(Have I totally surrendered to the flesh? What would have happened to the Jewish nation if Moses had access to a vibrating recliner? Would Caleb have been as sure of his power to overcome the natives of the promised land? Or would they simply have decided to go rocking? In fact, is a vibrating recliner an addiction, calling for a 12-Step program?) No, now that I am in Christ I must die to the flesh, and have God working through me. But I think he works through me very well when I'm reclining.

Chapter XXXIII

I Want to Please God

When I was little, I wanted to please my parents. I loved them and their love caused me to obey them. From age 3 to age 12, I was pretty much an ideal child. I got good grades, which was very important to them. With their approval I stayed close to home, spending happy hours in my spacious and private back yard listening to the St. Louis Cardinals play baseball on the portable radio. During the World Series, I took the radio to school—even though it weighed some 20 pounds and I weighed 60! I made few demands, and was grateful for the things I got from them at Christmas and birthdays. When I got to be junior high and high school age I was less sensitive to my mother and dad, but as a child I was intent on making them happy with me.

That's how I try to be with God today. As a baby in Christ, I keep in contact with prayer. I give thanks daily for all his blessings. I really try to live in perpetual gratitude.. I work for the kingdom, both in his church and in my daily life with my writing. I know that God created the universe and is the embodiment of truth, and that is the God that stays uppermost in my mind to write about, and talk about.

Today, I got out my hammer and opened some hazelnuts as I thought about this chapter. One particularly resistant nut required repeated beatings, and a thought came to me, "that was a tough nut to crack," a metaphor my

parents often employed to describe a person of their acquaintance. I guess the reason that sprang to mind was that
I was the original tough nut to crack. All my life I had been
resisting committing myself to Jesus. I did it once in 1978
in the Episcopal church, but fell away. I did it again last
year, when I was 68 years old! Talk about resistance.

But like the daily and hourly workers in the vineyard,
all of whom got a dinnarius, I got just as much grace as did
my friend Earl, who came to Christ on a battleship in World
War II. To me, that is just one more reason to love Jesus,
and do my best to please him. He does, after all, really please
me. Pastor Brian Broderson, one of my heroes, points out
that God is really very reasonable. The only things God
calls us to do injure us if we don't obey. A person's god is
their master passion, he says quoting his pastor Chuck
Smith. And sometimes that results in putting other gods
ahead of God. That's idolatry, he says. "God wants us to be
passionate about him, for him to be the master passion of
our lives," he adds. (www.calvarybasics.org)

Chapter XXXIV

Ministers, All

Today my Bible gave me even more motivation to complete this little tome. It must be my angel, who is inspiring me when my resolve is flagging, who led me to this passage 1 Peter 2:9; "But you are a chosen people, a royal priesthood, a holy nation a people belonging to God, that you may declare the praises of him who called you out of darkness into his wonderful light." Peter, writing to believers, tells us all that we are a royal priesthood. Pastor Jon Courson of Calvary Chapel of Costa Mesa has a radio show (www.searchlightradio.org) which examines this passage, saying that even if believers are plumbers, they are ministers, and that at Wal-Mart we are all to behave as Christians should behave.

So I have a Biblical imprimatur (I am a minister, too) to continue this work. In fact, I'm supposed to do it; God wants me to. No wonder that angel is so helpful! As it says in Romans, I am to offer myself a living sacrifice to God, and that means I hope my eyes see as he sees and my heart accepts as he accepts. When I go to sing this morning with the "Over 55 Singers" at a nursing home in Carlsbad, I want my resolve to be God's resolve to help the residents and make them joyful. I'm turning over my vocal chords to God. (The other alto is tied up with jury duty, so my vocal chords need all the help they can get.)

In the End, It's Faith

One of my greatest joys in my work in Alcoholics Anonymous has been to be around a long time; I've seen hopeless addicts turn their lives around and become successful citizens. It's like the kick I got in my English classes when even the most dense students "got it" and understood what literature was all about. I guess I'm just a transformation junkie, because giving someone the gospel message and seeing their lives redirected is a similar kick. I simply love it, even though my experience with prosytlyzing is limited. There is a qualitative difference: In AA I can save a life in and save a mind in teaching but to turn someone to Christ gives them eternity. What a gift!

Yessir, work in the ministry is rewarding, no matter what branch of the ministry I'm talking about. Earlier today, it was bringing the traditional old hymns to a roomful of nursing home residents. We were enthusiastic singers, making up for only moderate expertise, and all the ladies and gentlemen seemed to really enjoy singing with us. Something about The Old Rugged Cross (it is requested every time) and In the Garden touches hearts whether young or old. Both those songs, and all the others, touch my heart, too. What a joy it is to sing them.

Chapter XXXV

Do I Have a Leading?

The Apostle Paul, writing under the influence of the Holy Spirit, tells us we must die to self and live for Jesus. On the other hand, America's prevailing wisdom seems to be that we should love ourselves first, then we can love others. We should strengthen our egos and firmly establish our boundaries, and then we can turn our attention to relating to others. Popular psychology and sociology leave Jesus out of the equation; they tell us to put ourselves first, not last. Self sacrifice is defined as co-dependence and yes, there is a 12-Step program for that. Goads from children's books to Oprah emphasize "doing something nice for ourselves".

One of my most successful (in terms of life, career, relationships, marriage, etc.) friends looks at herself in the mirror every morning and says "Hello, beautiful. What can I do to make you happy today?" In my contrary way, I ask God every morning to encourage me to conform to his will and to do what is right for him and my friends. Usually, as in the case of this chapter, God gives me a "leading" and I have the joy of accomplishment at the end of the day.

I know people who "put themselves out" for others much more than I do. My growth group leader Carol visited me when I was sick last year, as did my hostess for the group, Joni. Both brought me food and it was a great blessing for me. Carol brought a bottle of "pills" which were rolled up Bible verses in capsules; she had typed, rolled, and inserted them herself. Joni, the embodiment of a green thumb, brought flowers. Both these ladies inspired me to be a more caring friend. I confess to getting busy with my own projects and not being as unselfish as I wish I were. If my actions aren't always ok, my intentions are. Now, if I could just "pump up" my character and do what I know is right! Paul had trouble with that one, too, writing that he did what he didn't want to do and didn't do what he did want to do. (My spiritual advisor, Tom, wanted me to re-think this passage, telling me that Jesus justified Paul and that I shouldn't "pump up" my character but surrender to the Holy Spirit and let him change me. Do you see why I respect his judgment? He even made me re-read Romans 7:15)

I try to keep in mind that we have all sinned and fallen short of the Glory of God and that we don't deserve the Grace he has given us. I am entitled to eternal life simply by acknowledging what Jesus has done for me. With that astonishing truth, why wouldn't I try to die to self, to quash my self-centeredness?(1 Corinthians 15:31) Why wouldn't I put God first? Are my "boundaries" all that important? What can I do to make God happy today?

It is true, not everything we do in this country makes God happy. I'm sure our soft-porn movies and hard-core pornography internet sites make him weep; I'm sure that America's preoccupation with pleasure and ease and comfort are hard for God to approve of. The places where the Bible isn't welcome must tax God's good will. Murder, child molestation, frivolous law suits, money-grubbing televangelists, abortion, euthanasia, capital punishment, the list of thorns in God's side is legion.

Do I Have a Leading?

We shrug, as good Christians, and say "that's just how it is." The question is, how have we allowed it to happen? What can we do? Is our moral rot so extensive that we really are "the great Satan?" That's a terrible, terrible thought.

Chapter XXXVI

On Lies and Lying

My handy little paperback, *Find it Fast in the Bible* by Ron Rhodes is a kind of mini-concordance that gives the Word a once-over lightly. Today I caught myself in two lies, and I looked up lies and liars in *Find it*. Sixteen verses led me to Psalms, Proverbs, Acts, Revelation, John, and Colossians. All indicated lying is a very bad thing, saying that those who do it are headed for hell and even in one case (Psalm 55:23) that liars will die young. Fortunately, I have avoided the latter and hope that I am not going to hell, thank you very much. God forgives much, I know.

It doesn't take a lot of Biblical knowledge to figure out that God doesn't like liars. One of my friends in sharing her testimony said that a propensity toward lying led her to repent and come to Christ when a Christian friend told her "God hates liars." (Whatever it takes is whatever it takes.)

My lies today (I think) were both excuses, and both of them were unnecessary and fell into the category of "recreational lying." When I took my laundry in to be washed, dried, and folded, I told the worker that I was out of time to do it myself (which was true) and that I was going out of town. The last-mentioned was a lie. She didn't deserve to be lied to, even though she didn't seem to be listening. Because I haven't died young and my short-term memory is history I don't remember the exact circumstances surrounding the second example. I recall it made me feel somewhat awful when I did it, and I think it was probably another excuse. I don't know. But I asked forgiveness for each of these tiny transgressions and feel I probably got it.

When I was little, I lied constantly. So did my mother. I comforted myself that it ran in the family, and with the age-old conviction that if my mother did it, it was all right. The very first day in Kindergarten I told the teacher it was ok for me to get orange juice instead of milk, a report that was made up of whole cloth. It was downhill from there.

Two years ago now, when I gave my life to Jesus, I included in my dedication (a very private matter) that I wouldn't sin any more, and that meant, among many other things, that I wouldn't lie.

"We are all sinners and have fallen short of the Glory of God" was the verse (Romans 3:23) that made me aware that I couldn't lie (among many other things) any more. On the whole, with most of the "other things" I have been successful. With lying I am still struggling. Those prevarications flow from my tongue so easily!

My problem appears to be a metaphysical one. I hate lying. I should love truth. When I say "don't lie," what my conscience hears is "lie," and if I said "love truth" that would be healthier. I can put Philippians 4:8 on a card and read it over and over: "Fix your thoughts on what is true." Incidentally, *Find it* lists 21 references for the word "truth." Since there were 16 for "liars" this is accentuating the positive.

That's good advice for me, as well. If I am serious about this "Living to Please God" stuff, I darn well better focus on truth instead of lying.

Chapter XXXVII

Meat Instead of Milk

The first year that Christ was in my heart, I read everything I could about Christianity. I read all of Max Lucado, all of Philip Yancey, all of Lee Strobel, I read books by Bill Hybels and a host of others. The Holy Spirit was goading me on to read everything I could about my new beliefs. I couldn't get enough. My two devout daughters gave me the Mitford books and others and introduced me to Christian fiction as well as commentary. I even read a parable Nina recommended, *Hinds Feet in High Places*.

I was like a person consulting his elders. I had no perspective of my own—this was my attempt to gain some. And I did, I guess. I knew how to answer some skeptics, I grew in devotion to God. Most of all, I became teachable about the meaning of the Word.

Then Tom, my growth group leader and spiritual advisor ,presented me with a lesson : "Stop reading about Jesus and read what he said, how he fulfilled prophecy, how his message was brought to the world. Read your Bible."

Because I was a fledgling, I first treated my Bible like the I Ching. I opened and read it, expecting God to speak to me. One of my radio pastors, I think Chuck Smith, tells the story of a man who did that and opened the Word and it said "then Judas hanged himself." Turning again, he found "Go thou and do likewise." I soon began to read my Bible on a systematic basis, and Pastor Larry and my growth group had us all ranging through scripture. To do our weekly growth group homework, we had to read illustrative verse after illustrative verse. Often, we had to choose which of a group of verses spoke most loudly to us. As we turned weekly to the scriptures, Larry knew what he was doing; he was giving us meat instead of milk.

This regimen of weekly thumbing through the Bible did wonders for my Biblical literacy. Often, Proverbs, Psalms, Esther, are cited on my favorite radio pastors and I read them through. Larry spoke about 1 Kings this week, and a blank patch in my reading was opened to me. I confess to skipping text here and there.

When I repented and gave my life to Jesus, my daughter in Maine sent me a Bible, the NIV version. I had only been familiar with the King James, which I read for its literary value, and I was pleased with the ease of comprehension I found in the NIV. Since it was easier for me to read, I read it more often. And since I read it more often, it spoke to me more and more. And I understood more and more. What a happy circumstance.

I am convinced, now, that those people who say that Jesus was a great teacher but no more divine than you and I simply haven't read the Bible. I wrote in an earlier book that Proverbs is better than T. Berry Brazelton for child rearing, and last night Larry spoke to Solomon's advice about "Love and faithfulness or responsibility" being the two essentials of a leader, whether he be a king or a nursery school teacher. I reflected that had been true in my experience, whether as a sorority president or an editor.

Today, I marvel at the thousands of lessons for my life found in the Bible. I'm very glad I read about God, and now I'm very glad I read his word. I'm a lot better for it.

Chapter XXXVIII

God's Great Gifts

My heavenly father is continually surprising me. He did that twice today, once at a 6:30 a.m. meeting and again at noon. The earlier instance was a discussion of spiritual awakenings, whether they were immediate or gradual, and whether they were gifts. One noteworthy speaker said he couldn't see them as gifts, I expect because he is agnostic in his outlook and a gift implies a giver. When it was my turn, out of my mouth came the following, through no volition of my own: "If I live in gratitude, then I can perceive almost everything as a gift, whether good or bad. God tells me in the Bible that his ways are not my ways and that he has his own time frame for things, thanks very much. With a strong sense of God, everything is a blessing." Now we don't usually get into matters like this in the meeting, and I detected some approbation. But I didn't really figure that out, God did. And since it came through my heart to my tongue, I expect that at least for me it is really, truly right. I am extremely grateful, especially for ideas like that one.

The second surprise came at a noon meeting when I flashed back to a period of excessive drinking and remembered wandering through my empty house with a glass in my hand, despairing "I couldn't drink any more, and I couldn't not drink" was how God prompted me, and while that may have been a canard to many, it was a brand new thought to me. Somewhere in that pronouncement I called God "my heavenly father" which I do when talking to myself but do rarely in public.

The Apostle Paul wrote that "he was not ashamed of the gospel of Christ"(Romans 1-16) and I guess my initial feelings of reticence are giving way to a bolder style. I was surprised again.

I have always loved ideas, and have picked them up willy-nilly like some collectors of certain objects; the best ideas, however, come straight from God who is often dealing out happy surprises to me. With those usually comes delight, and with delight, heightened gratitude, and with gratitude, more frequent happy surprises. Since this book, in a humble way, is a collection of those ideas, those surprises, then the more of them I have the longer this will be. And, incidentally, the more strengthened in my faith I will become.

I know Jesus died for me, bringing me salvation and eternity in heaven; that he was and is the propitiation for my sins, which I daily commit. The apostle Paul said at the beginning of his ministry that he was "the lowest of the apostles," then later the lowest of the saints, and finally he was characterizing himself as a terrible sinner. The closer he got to God, the more clearly he saw himself. In 1 Timothy 1:15 he called himself the greatest of all sinners.

I can see him in jail, writing to his churches, and know how absolutely delighted he was when God gave him a fine turn of phrase. We writers exult in such things. I can't compare myself to Paul in any way other than craftsmanship; he was a missionary unparalleled in history. But we both called on God a lot.

So Paul's words in the Bible are God's words. I wish for mine that they would strike a chord or two in my readers and listeners. Maybe it will help that goal since I'm finally giving credit where credit is due. Thank you, Lord.

Chapter XXXIX

Servant Leadership

If ever I needed a boost about God's Miracle working power, I needed it this week. Feeling unworthy of having any mission to write *"Living to Please God"*, I sent for Calvary Chapel founder Chuck Smith's book, *Harvest* about the unlikely crew of drug dealers, criminals, followers of the occult, and demon-possesed men who spread his church throughout America and into Europe.

In the largest explosion of religion since Millard Filmore began the Unity movement in the 1920's, Calvary burst upon the American scene in the 1970s as an alienated generation came to Jesus. Chronicling the testimonies of the men I listen to on the Calvary Network every day, Smith modestly describes his work in their lives, and gives the credit to God. Well, that's where the credit belongs, all right, but God needs henchmen and Smith is one without parallel.

Only a few of these church leaders, who have built some of the largest congregations in North America, have theological training. All learned the Bible at Smith's Calvary Chapel Costa Mesa, one of the three largest churches in the country. Raul Reis, I learned to my surprise, is the best educated, but he wears it well. As I mentioned above, it is his enthusiasm for Jesus that impressed me. Incidentally, Reis could hardly read when he first came to Christ. Now he has three college degrees, one of them a doctorate.

Also, after reading the profiles of Smith's men, I was not surprised when Jon Courson, also mentioned above, was called back to Costa Mesa to take Smith's place, presumably. Smith describes Courson as a man's man and a dying breed, one who was raised to be a football captain, a valedictorian, Most Likely to Succeed, and an outstanding young man who won a scholarship to Biola Christian college. Courson's life long Christianity is in stark contrast to the early drugging, alcohol, and crimes of some of his minister-peers. Because his life reflects Smith's own upbringing, Courson and Smith are like father and son. I listen to them exegete the Bible together on "To Every Man an Answer" on the Calvary network, and they are an unbeatable team, and clearly warm friends. Courson obviously respects Smith enormously, but is not silent when he disagrees with his mentor. Courteously, he will give a different answer to a questioner. An example would be yesterday's question about what Paul meant when he wrote "I die daily." Smith said it was because every day he faced death, a conclusion I disagreed with. Courson gave the answer I was thinking of: Dying to the old man and taking on a life of faith, a life in the Body of Christ. Who on earth am I to disagree with Chuck Smith? I was pretty worried until Courson spoke up.

I spend endless hours listening to these minister's thoughts. In my car, in my kitchen, and when I go to bed at night I sop them up like a thirsty sponge. I guess I'm a typical new Christian, reveling in the Honeymoon. I'm grateful I know so much about these disembodied radio voices, now. Thanks to *Harvest,* I'm on a new footing with these guys. And I'm even more convinced of God's miracle working power .I know now that I'm a combination of Jon Courson and Raul Reis and that's probably why they both speak so clearly to me. Do you think God can do with me what he did with them? I'm praying it is so.

Chapter XL

Pronunciation in the Body of Christ

This chapter came to me this morning after the prayer at the 6:30 a.m. meeting. Half the people said A men, as in hay. The other half said ahmen, as in shaw. I've noticed this division before. Some pray-ers are adamant A meners, and they tend to be louder than their "ah" compatriots. I don't know why. I'm an ah mener myself, and I guess since I'm not sure I'm right, I let others drown me out, volume-wise. Maybe the A meners are sure they're right, and that accounts for it.

But that isn't all. At the end of the Lord's prayer, some churchgoers end it with "forever." Another group say "for ever and ever." Now once upon a time there was an inventive professor at Harvard named Tom Lehrer who described his math students as "those who graduated from high school before (was in 1940?) and between those who went to private and public schools." Those factors determined how students divided and multiplied in some way now lost to me, but I suspect high church and low church backgrounds account for this prayer difference, and even possibly a date or so. Or perhaps it is geographical. I know Easterners, of whom I was once one, pronounce all kinds of thing differently than I now do as a Westerner. I grew up in Kansas, and learned there to talk through my nose, I believe. I also had great difficulty with "our" words. Tour was "ter." I remembered that at my 50th high school reunion when we planned a "ter" and I didn't know what it was. (How quickly we forget.)

Another illustration lost to memory is a series of words that identified one from being native to a region of the US. Some of them must have ended in "r" as such words end in "ah" in Boston, Maine, and New Hampshire and sometimes in Rhode Island. Ouse words differentiate Canadians from U.S. natives. Canadians say "hoose." I believe another differentiation was possible with roof. Westerners, as I recall, rhyme it with ruff. Easterners say "ruef."

Now that we have 12 hours of TV programming a week for the average child, maybe this georgraphical imprinting will be a thing of the distant past, as announcers and actors tend to have accentless delivery.

But the chance that these children will watch Christian television is so slight that the A men, Ah men division will probably continue. Ditto for the "forever" and "for ever and ever" schism; it will still be standard operating procedure.

I'm pretty positive the last word that diagnosed differences was "sure." New Yorkers say "shuwuh" making it two syllables, and those Midwesterners say "sher." I dimly remember there was a Baltimore pronunciation of something that identified a native. I think it was saying sure as sure. How prosaic!

Chapter XLI

Living Biblically

I think God celebrates with cake and candles when one of his children turns to the Word to solve a living problem, or otherwise make a decision. I always know that when I do that, God is pleased. He says so. "Blessed are those who hear and obey," Luke 11:28; "Let the word of Christ dwell in you," Colossians 3:16, Psalm 119, Hebrews 4:12. 13: the Word of God is living."

My once-over lightly concordance lists three pages of passages for adversity, prayers in adversity, and why God allows adversity. I could add bulk to this tome if I cited every one of them, but surely this sample shows God has many, many uses for his Word. Psalm 119 is the best example: "You have laid down precepts that are to be fully obeyed; oh, that my ways were steadfast in obeying your decrees." Verse 4 and 5. "How can a young man keep his way pure? By living according to your word." Verse 9. "Your statutes are my delight; they are my counselors. Verse 24. All of psalm 119 continues in its paean to the word of God.

We can purge sinfulness by dwelling in the word; we can face adversity when dwelling in the word. We can learn to live a Godly life by dwelling in the word.

Little wonder that Bible-teaching churches such as mine are growing by leaps and bounds. After years of experience teachings and relevance teachings, religion in America seems to be returning to the Bible truths that all people have hungered for, from B.C. to the millennium. I think the tide turned when radio stations like Chuck Smith's KWVE had as their calling to "teach the Word of God. Teach only the Word of God." For many hours a day, his Calvary Chapel band of brothers does just that. It truly is a "Wave of Living Water."

I'm so fortunate that I have the Calvary network programs I have. I thank God for my move to California, and know that it happened as God wanted so I could grow in my love for him.

Chapter XLII

A Higher IQ

I have long accepted, even when not a Christian, that there is a God and he is smarter than I am. That didn't take much getting used to. After all, even if he didn't create the universe, he's more accomplished than I am. (This was all BHS, or Before Holy Spirit). Now I am positively awed at the notion of God, the Holy Spirit, and Jesus. I recreate the old falling prostrate before him, though mentally.

But nobody told me when I got my Phi Beta Kappa key that someday my radio, my satellite dish, my computer, and even my porch light would outdo me.

As an aside, I have a friend who has a talking microwave. Since he lives alone, he programs replies into it. For example, he often says he is being harassed by members of his homeowner's association, so he turns to his microwave, pushes a button, and it says to him "you're so sensitive." Of course, he's put that in memory in the first place, but that doesn't make it any less consoling. I find these conversations really rather charming.

Back to my radio. Because it has multiple buttons on its sleek top, most of them with many functions depending on whether they are operating singly or in tandem with others in complex combinations, it turns on at 3 a.m. I simply can't dissuade it from doing this, no matter how many buttons I push. Fortunately, I often want to get up and work at

3 a.m. and there is no one to bother if I do. I harbor a secret worry that I am boring my future readers. In fact, I often worry there will be no future readers. Here's where I need a microwave that tells me I'm the best author since Philip Yancey.

My satellite dish often requires my hand to make it work. I shudder when the screen is filled with black and white oscillating boxes. Out comes the smart card, out comes the receiver with all its choices, and after fiddling I call the company and get guided through a fix. I never remember how I did it. It happens again and again.

Of course I'm less capable than my computer. I bought one and tried to learn to use it in '94. Sometime that year I was solicited by AOL to be a community leader in the Addiction and Recovery Forum. In my training periods I was so incompetent that I qualified for extra tutoring. Eventually I got the hang of some of the requirements, but I'll never forget the!!!!s I got when I answered the age question that I was 61. It seemed everyone else was 17. I've been through three computers since then, and my latest is a laptop that just fits in my tiny trailer. Out of its keys have come two books and multiple newspaper stories, so it fulfills its purpose, but every now and then it still gets the best of me.

That is because it has idiosyncrasies which I am now used to, rather like an eccentric husband (and I know whereof I speak). My word program, long installed, has quirks that would have driven a less patient person batty. The curser has a mind of its own, and often skips up or down, correcting and inserting at the wrong place. Constant attention to the screen is called for, and that's a pain when I am trying to quote a long passage.

Also, Stephen (my computer is named Stephen because it is a Dell and Stephen is the guy who says "Dude, you're getting a dell.") has a shift key that is uncomfortably close to the control key and the slightest miscalculation can result in disaster, as in paragraphs disappearing. Once, a book disappeared. Fortunately I had sent my daughter in Maine a copy and she was able to send it to me.

As for my porch light, my exemplary son-in-law, he of the birthday recliner, has installed and programmed that. My excuse is that it is far too high above my head to deal with.

It's way over my head, all right. They all are.

Chapter XLIII

Women and Evangelism

The late Mother Teresa refused to evangelize anyone. She once told the press that if her patient was a Hindu, she tried to make them a better Hindu, or ditto if they were Buddhist. This attitude seems to be endemic in today's world, after lessons learned with indigenous peoples who were converted to Christ, sometimes to their detriment. When the Indians in Central America were converted, they often became lost without their religious traditions and rituals and often turned to alcohol to heal the hurt. The same happened to the indigenous people in North America some three centuries later.

The modern world view that all roads lead to God—a view that I espoused in my first book—is just, I believe, patently false. Jesus made it plain over and over again that he was the Way, and that his death resolved the sin and death of all who believe in him. When we accept him that leads to our God, and that is the only road.

When I submitted my first book, *Turn Your Eyes* to a trusted editor, she warned me that people wouldn't like being told that their spiritual view was wrong if it didn't agree with mine. I'm prepared for that. Jesus said we would be reviled if we were followers. I'm afraid I've lost a friend or two already. Most, however, just chalk my love for the Lord up to a softened brain in the California sun.

In the End, It's Faith

My Maine daughter, Nina, two years ago went to Connecticut to hear a Women of Faith conference, and since she is an A plus evangelist, and was evangelized herself by Nancy, her sister, she loved it and felt confirmed in her faith. I would bet that almost all of the women who attend those programs are believers, though. Nina bought the tapes for her church and plays them for believers and non believers on her little island in Maine once a year. Food, from her mostly organic kitchen, sweetens the deal. I would guess that Nina rarely misses an opportunity to witness for the Lord.

But most of my believing friends are like I was: shy about it. Paul writes that he is not ashamed of the gospel of Jesus Christ, found as I wrote earlier in Romans 1:16.. I have missed many opportunities to witness about my faith, because I'm afraid that people will think me a raving zealot. Or that others will be offended by my convictions, or that "don't talk religion or politics" canard. I'm sure I should be about my Father's business. My savior said so. The great commission is "Go and spread the Gospel throughout the world" and that includes to Buddhists and Hindus. This tiny book is my attempt to make up for my verbal reticence. Over a long lifetime, I have noticed that women don't like confrontation, and evangelism usually involves a little bit of that. "Do you believe that Jesus died for your sins?" is pretty confrontational, at least as I see it.

Maybe that is why most pastors are men. Men like to fix things, and making a believer out of a non-believer is fixing them. Would that I were better at it, myself.

Chapter XLIV

Taking Gifts Seriously

"Oh, I couldn't do that" was my battle cry for years. It didn't matter what the circumstances, my disbelief in myself and my capabilities kept me in bondage.

Jesus fixed that. If my abilities are from accepting him and being taken over by the Holy Spirit, then I should use them, especially for his greater glory.

I have written about the Holy gall it took to write a Christian book when those much more qualified that I are producing works to glorify the Lord. I mentioned the fact that *Turn Your Eyes* was one of 100,000 Christian books written last year. Most of these authors are steeped in the Word and schooled in theology. All I have going for me is the fact that I love the Lord. I am truly a joyous Christian who is so excited about this new life that my fingers just race over my keyboard. That isn't exactly a qualification for writing. But it's all I have.

I guess I should take whatever gifts God has given me and use them, not forgetting to give him the glory. I've got to be like the ants described in the scripture who work diligently, even though they are unsupervised. (Proverbs 6:6). A speaker today on the Calvary network said we should work out in our spiritual gym, dedicating our time to God and the work he would have us do. He said that made one a happy Christian. Right!! I may not be Phillip Yancey, but at least I'm one of those gleeful followers of Christ. Halleluiah.

Chapter XLV

Happy Campers Inc.

I think those of us who are happy in our Christian life should form a society, even a union. Since I take care of a semi-disabled friend, and get paid for that by the state of California, I am a member of the United Domestic Workers of America of the AFL-CIO. (In the same mail that brought my UDWA newsletter came the Phi Beta Kappa Key Reporter. I wonder if my new mailman is mystified!)

I get some perks from my Union membership including effective lobbying at the legislature. In the face of terrible budget deficits in our state, I got a $1 an hour raise this year.

I would like to be the designated lobbyist for the Union of Happy Christians. I would appoint a committee of pastors I admire to evangelize the cabinet and legislature, to tell them about our happy life in Jesus. With that accomplished, laws would easily pass to restore prayer to the schools, to teach abstention in sexual life in our schools, and to discourage abortion. (I wouldn't criminalize it; too many women die when it's a criminal offense, getting back-alley abortions.) I certainly would emphasize adoption and teach the many terrible effects of an abortion on a woman's psyche. I'd put the consequences for the mother and father of such a death right up there on the Radar screen and see that it was taught.

I'd sing hymns in school, too. That was how I learned that Jesus was my redeemer and that he died for me. Amazing Grace and How Great Thou Art would be sung in school programs. Church –related clubs could meet and evangelize in schools. And since our leaders would be Christians, and therefore admirable, our laws would be fair and just. The general good of a rule would be the criteria, not pleasing a donor or special interest group.

Whoops, I think I'd have my $1 an hour raise repealed.

Chapter XLVI

Proving We Love God

While driving home from the jury pool today I heard an inspiring message from Calvary Pastor Greg Laurie which fits right into my thinking and my book, so I paid special attention. Laurie was discussing the recomissioning of Peter after he had denied the Lord three times the night of the crucifixion. In this section of Acts, Jesus asks Peter "do you love me?"

Laurie said, "What is the evidence that We love Jesus?" We should demonstrate by longing to know him personally, to have a close relationship, and that means by praying. We must have an active prayer life.

We should be eager to read God's Word. Like church-going, another indicator, the Word should be sought out daily, and meditated upon. We should love good, as God defines it in his law, and hate evil.

Hate has a place in the believer's pantheon, Laurie said. Citing the psalms, he says we mustn't regard as good those act and opinions that God has condemned. When we are enthralled by a television series which promotes evil thoughts or deeds, we are not loving God.

We should long for the return of Jesus. We must every day hope this is the day he will come and establish his kingdom.

And, of course, we should keep his commandments.

If we do these things, they are evidence that we love Jesus very much, that we are his true disciples.

I think I'm batting close to 500 here, and that most Christians are—at least the ones I know best. When I consider churchgoing, I am thrilled to do it and benefit every time. Laurie added that we should look forward to giving, however, and I am not there yet. I want to help the Lord's work and try to be a cheerful and generous parishioner but I see my tithing as a duty, not as a pleasure. Now that I've thought about it, I'll pray to change.

I can't tell the reader how many times I've heard people say that they love God but hate the church, or they hate Christians. Now I know that some of my brothers and sisters can be irritating and even arrogant, but these are the body of Christ, and I cut their personalities a lot of slack. We are all in the Kingdom together, and I love them.

A Godly love will, in time, foster being humble and being teachable, and that's how I see these people in the long run. God is still working on them, or, as in the case of the little story, he isn't finished with them yet. They are to be gently corrected, not hated.

I'm reminded every week by Pastor Larry that Jesus will take the steering wheel of my life, forgive my sins, adopt me into his family, and change me from the inside out. As Greg Laurie says, I love the Lord and wish to be in his company, both now and in eternity. I love reading the Word. I am now repulsed by my former bad habits or evil ways and wish to avoid them at all costs. Blessedly, most of them aren't even tempting any more. If I am tempted, I pray to have that temptation neutralized with great success. Praying is, after all, also evidence that we love God as Laurie says.

Do I love my neighbor as myself? I do love myself, although that took a long long time after years of disappointing myself. There is a neighbor here and there that I don't love, however, if "neighbor" is defined as another person I'm in proximity with. In my class I teach at the Adult Center, there is an irritating young woman who tries my patience. I'm praying for her, too. If I do that for about three weeks, things will change, I believe. That's an instance of something I wrote earlier: I advise my friends to do that, so I darn well better do it, too. Resentment gives others rent in my head, is the saying. Besides, it isn't a very Christian thing to do to resent another.

The upshot of all this is that I'm checking myself against Laurie's list as a sure index that I'm headed in the right direction, spiritually.

If you'd like to hear this wonderful minister, his web site is www.Harvest.org. For that matter, my minister, Larry Osborne, is at www.northcoastchurch.org. Both of them are really first class teachers of the Word.

Chapter XLVII

Standing in the Gap

I probably would still be skimming along in my materialist, humanist way if it were not for my daughters Nancy and Nina. They prayed me into the Kingdom, I'm sure. Nancy came to Christ first, then convicted Nina, and they both convicted me. I figured that if these two intelligent and sensible women believed the Bible and lived by its precepts, then I could try to do the same. All of us are standing in the gap for Carole, the third daughter, and believing that in time she will join us. If it was done for me, then I can do it for her. I pray this works. I want her to have the life and peace and joy that Paul talks about, that I have a great deal of the time.

Like the instance of the recliner, where the good might have been enemy of the best, Carole's circumstances are good. She tells me she is happy and I believe she is. It is hard for her to see that she might be even happier.

The best is life with Jesus. There just isn't any better.

My growth group is praying for Carole as well, and Nina reports that her little church in Sunshine, Maine is adding to the chorus. That church is really effective. They prayed for me.

Last week, Tom, my growth group leader and spiritual advisor, reported that when he and daughter Nancy were in the same group in a former church, Nancy had asked him to pray for me, and he had. I'll bet Tom has stood in the gap for hundreds over his long life in the Lord. We currently pray for children of growth group members, including Carole.

With all this heavenly power focused on her from East and West coasts, do you think Carole can continue to hold out? I pray she can't.

Chapter XLVIII

Heeding Authority

An interesting phenomenon has occurred as I write for the daily newspaper, here. Let's backtrack: For ten years I was the editor or was lightly edited at best in Oviedo, FL. Further, I had to grind out several stories a week with little time for polishing.

Now, I have an experienced and exacting editor in Michael who initially had little confidence in me. After all, I am a bit long in the tooth and he is young with the typical jaundiced eye toward seniors.

As time goes on, I have written more and more for Michael's standards—with an eye toward his requirements, which it took me about four months to learn. He is increasingly happy with me, sending an email on the last story that it was an "excellent job." Do you see where I am heading with this notion?

For much of my life I was my own ultimate authority. When I left my parents' home and married, I'm afraid I didn't very often defer to my husband. (That was probably a factor in our divorce.) In my editorial jobs I didn't often consult others. In volunteer activities, I was like a bull in a china shop, plowing ahead and damn the torpedoes, to mix metaphors.

Well, you say, how can it be that you have altered your attitude? What made you submit to Michael's standards? Ah, the key is the word "submit." I got used to not being my own woman when I signed on to conversion almost two years ago. If I consider God on matters, it's not much of a reach to consider Michael.

And just as I get a "well done" from above when a decision or task goes smoothly, I really feel good about checking in with a higher power. I have an example: My move to California. The cross-country drive was loads of fun. The 5th Wheel I live in is great. I adore my daughter and her family. I love my life here. The move came after my decision for Christ and as I prayed over the decision, it seemed right. I even came out to Vista and tried it out for two months before I closed my apartment and packed my car and moved for good. When "all my lights are green," then I know it's a God thing. When there is obstacle after obstacle, I've done the wrong thing. It isn't God-approved. At least, that's how it seems.

Back to Michael. I'm really very fond of him and consider him a fine writer. I don't mind deferring to his judgment. In fact, it makes me a better reporter. Just as deferring to Jesus makes me a better person.

Is this a parable? Yep, with interpretation.

Chapter XL°IX

Receiving

In Christianity, there is lots of "receiving" going on.

First and foremost, we have to receive salvation, believing that Jesus died for us, or as Calvary Pastor Greg Laurie put it, "he paid a debt he did not owe because we had a debt we could not pay." Dear Earle of my growth group tells us that at 80 after more than 60 years since giving his life to Christ, he still sins every day. Me, too. I catch myself in prevaricating (sounds better than lying) almost daily. God is "the way, the truth, and the light," I know he wants me to be truthful to follow him. I still fall short.

Since Jesus gave us grace, we have to receive that, too. Our sins are forgiven because he loved us and died for us, not because we did anything. Grace is a gift. We have to thank him, live in gratitude, and, as above, receive.

He loves us, and is our shield, refuge, and glory. More receiving.

Because I know so little, I think receiving is the result of an open heart. Those who are closed up and self-sufficient don't seem to be very good at accepting the gifts that Jesus so sweetly offers. The broken ones have a clear channel to their hearts.

Jesus' conscription of humble men to be his disciples tells us that the proud and accomplished are not his first choice for followers. As in the case of the rich young man, there are many barriers to receiving his message.

The correctness of Jesus' choices was shown when almost all the original disciples died early martyr's deaths after bringing thousands to Christ. (John lived to a ripe old age, but he was the only one.)

I can't help but make the parallel between the early disciples and the throng of young ministers that came from Calvary Chapel Costa Mesa here in Southern California. This unlikely band, which has also brought thousands to Jesus, has formed a loose denomination of Christianity all by themselves. Greg Laurie just gave a 30th anniversary sermon in which he quoted David's last words to his son, Solomon. (1 Kings 1,2.) Laurie is just one of hundreds of servants of Christ who was loved into service by Calvary Chapel of Costa Mesa and its minister, Chuck Smith.

Have you received the Gospel? Do you believe that Jesus died for you? If you do, receive him into your open heart. As my dear minister Larry says, he'll change you from the inside out, and you'll get daily doses of joy. That's a promise.

Chapter L

Finish Line

Well, who would have thought that my meager knowledge of the Bible and Christianity and Jesus and God would have stretched to 50 chapters! I am speechless. Fortunately, my computer is still going and I can still type. And I want to give God the glory, as usual, for guiding me through this effort. I am deeply grateful for all the gifts he has given me; for my being prolific, for my faith, for my desultory diligence in grinding out the copy , for my inspiration, and for the certainty that is what I should be doing. Ever since I worked on the Northland News, then Good News, Etc., both of them Christian publications, I have been sure that whatever talent I have to craft sentences should be applied to the Kingdom. Doing that is reward enough. Already a previous book has had some influence in the life of a friend, and it has only been out a few weeks.

The Great Commission: Jesus said go and spread the Gospel throughout the earth and I found a Mission Field in my own backyard, I believe. Fortunately, I am not called to go cohabitate with snakes and spiders in some faraway jungle. God seems to approve of my sitting in my comfortable trailer and writing. If I'm wrong about that, I'll learn it soon enough when nobody reads my books.

If this book spoke to you in any way, send a note to 3408 Fairview Drive, Vista, CA 92084. I'd love to reply.
God Bless You.
Letty Linhart

To order additional copies of

In the End, It's Faith

have your credit card ready and call:

800-917- BOOK (2665)

or visit our website at :

Printed in the United States
1073200003B

9 781589 300859